Hearing their Voices:
Teaching History to Students of Color

Kay Traille

ROWMAN & LITTLEFIELD
Lanham • Boulder • New York • London

Published by Rowman & Littlefield
A wholly owned subsidiary of The Rowman & Littlefield Publishing Group, Inc.
4501 Forbes Boulevard, Suite 200, Lanham, Maryland 20706
www.rowman.com

6 Tinworth Street, London, SE11 5AL, United Kingdom

Copyright © 2020 by Kay Traille

All rights reserved. No part of this book may be reproduced in any form or by any electronic or mechanical means, including information storage and retrieval systems, without written permission from the publisher, except by a reviewer who may quote passages in a review.

British Library Cataloguing in Publication Information Available

Library of Congress Cataloging-in-Publication Data Available

ISBN 978-1-4758-5555-5 (cloth)
ISBN 978-1-4758-5556-2 (pbk.)
ISBN 978-1-4758-5557-9 (electronic)

In memory of my mother, Leila Louise Weir Traille,
who gave me my love of history
And
To my students who have taught me to listen

Contents

Preface		xi
	Teaching History	xii
	The Author's Background	xii
	Collective Memory	xiv
	Theoretical Framework	xvi
	Organization of the Book	xvii
Acknowledgments		xix
Chapter 1	The History of History Education for African American Students Since 1800	1
	Antebellum Denial of African American Education	1
	Education Trends in the United States	2
	Black Codes	3
	Booker T. Washington and W. E. B. Du Bois	3
	Exclusionary Stories	5
	History Education	6
	Marcus Garvey and Black Consciousness	7

	Carter G. Woodson	8
	Education Since the *Brown v. Board of Education Topeka* Decision	8
	Sputnik and Education	9
	Deficit Cultures	9
	Title 1 and Head Start	10
	The Coleman Report	11
	Students Taking Center Stage	11
	Busing and Integration	12
	Legislation	12
	Bilingual Education (1968–2001)	12
	Title IX (1972)	12
	PL 94–142 (1975) Later Became Individuals with Disabilities Education Act (1991, 1997)	12
	A Nation at Risk (1983)	12
	No Child Left Behind (2001)	13
	In-Service and Pre-Service Teachers	14
	American Schools in the Twenty-First Century	15
Chapter 2	How Students Learn History and Why It Matters	17
	Why How Students Learn History Is Important	17
	Understanding Students' Thinking about History: Why Inclusive Narratives Are Important	18
	Teaching and Learning History	19
	How Students Make Sense of History	21
	African Americans and History Lessons	22
	Afrocentric Narratives	23
	Multiculturalism	25

Chapter 3	Cognitive and Affective Factors and Possible Impact on the Learning of Multicultural Students	29
	Extrinsic and Intrinsic Motivation	29
	Fearing Failure	30
	Motivational Processes	31
	The Nature of the Self-Concept	33
	Self-Concept and Self-Esteem	33
	Age and Self-Concept	34
	Self-Efficacy and Educational Attainment	35
	The Black Self-Concept	36
	Social Identity	37
	A Social Constructionist Perspective of Self	38
	The Role of Attitudes in Processing Learning	41
	Attitudes and Behavior	41
	Approaches for Encouraging Attitude Change	42
	Brain-Based Research	42
Chapter 4	Students of Color Talk About the Role and Purpose of History in Their Lives	45
	Fact Finding Interviews	45
	Talking About School History	45
	History Is for Helping Us Understand the Contemporary and a Guide for Future Action	46
	Memory	46
	History Is for Telling Us Who We Are or Can Be	48
	Possible Selves	49
	Hidden Histories	51
	History Is for Personal and Social Interest	53
	History Is for Personal and Social Knowledge	53
	Issues of Perspective and Historical Explanation	55

Chapter 5	Decoding Student's Ideas	59
	Student Profiles	59
	History Is Ideal	60
	History Is Satisfactory	60
	History Is Inadequate	61
	What We Dislike about History Lessons	63
	Loving and Loathing: Differences in Motivation	63
	Personal Interest	64
	Lack Of and Negative Representation	64
	Connecting and Disconnecting	65
	Discussing and Understanding	65
	Role-Play and Discussion	66
	Interest and Curiosity	67
	Likes and Dislikes	68
	Content and Teaching	69
	Teaching Methods and Strategies	69
	Doing History	69
	Pattern of Findings	70
	Responses from Black Students	71
	Conclusions	72
Chapter 6	Counterstories of American History: Students of Color Examine the Past	73
	Background	73
	Task 1 Nelson Mandela	74
	Task 2	75
	Task 1 Second World War	76
	Counterstories	77
	Silent Observers	79
	Setting and Participants	80

	Research Questions	80
	Counterstories of Native Nations: Students of Color	81
	White Students and Native Nations	83
	Counterstories of Slavery: Students of Color	85
	White Students and Slavery	87
	The Civil War	89
	Students of Color and White Students' Counterstories of Post–Civil War Life	90
	Discussion	90
Chapter 7	An Approach for Teaching World History	95
	Participants	96
	Context	96
	Baudolino, Fantasy or the Lying Historian	97
	Religion and Identity	102
	Origins	104
	Eurocentric "Exceptionalism"	104
	Alternative Narratives	105
	Eras	107
	Eurocentrism	108
	The Origins of the Modern World	108
	Differences in Students' Data	109
	Eras	109
	Conclusion	110
Chapter 8	Cultivating Curiosity, Complexity and Authentic Engagement in History Classrooms for Students of Color	113
	Prerequisites and Preparations	113
	Attitudes and Expectations of Educators	114
	Communication	115

	Building Relationships	116
	Linguistically Relevant and Responsive Pedagogy	117
	Families and Communities	118
	Activity—Classroom Climate	119
	Activity-Negotiating Expectations and Behaviors	120
	Reading and Writing	122
	Activity—Developing New Competencies	123
	Strategies and Methods	124
	Perspectives	125
	Digital Frameworks	126
	Identities and Social Groups	127
	Counterfactual and Complex Histories	129
	Black Consciousness and the Building and Protecting of America	129
	Slavery	130
	Activities—Collaborative Instruction	132
	Using Material Culture	133
	Activity—Testing With Less Fear	134
	In Summary	135
	Conclusion	136
Appendix		141
	Data Collection, Coding and Method of Analysis for Counterstories in Chapter 7	141
	Category Coding	141
	Categories and Indicators	142
References		143
Index		153
About the Author		163

Preface

Mali Empire; Empire of Ghana, Songhai Empire; Kanen-Bornu; Kingdom of Nri; Igboland; Oyo Empire; Ashanti Empire; Akan People; Kong Empire; Sokoto Caliphate; Empire of Kitara; Kongo Empire; Mutapa Empire; Sulu Kingdom; Kingdom of Kerma; Kingdom of Kush; Ancient Egypt; Banu Ifran Dynasty; Almoravid Dynasty; Kingdom of Askum; Ethiopian Empire; Arjuran Sultanate; Fulani, Jolof Empire; Benin; Hausa—histories, some half remembered, most forgotten or ignored.

Magna Carta; Christopher Columbus; Reformation; Pilgrim Fathers; Thirteen Colonies; Revolution; Independence; Constitution; Federalist Papers; George Washington; Thomas Jefferson; Westward Expansion; Andrew Jackson; Slavery; Abraham Lincoln; Civil War; Reconstruction; Industrial Revolution; Populists; Progressivism; First World War; Roaring Twenties; Wall Street Crash; Depression; Pearl Harbor; Second World War; Cold War—histories, most remembered, commemorated, celebrated.

Abenaki; Acatec; Aztec; Arapaho; Black Carib; Caddo; Cahita; Cayuga; Cowichan; Cheyenne; Chickasaw; Dakota; Erie; Fox; Hupa; Innu; Iroquois Confederacy; Powhatan; Jaqaru; Lushshootseed; Mobile; Nottoway; Oconee; Paiqueets; Ramamuri; Spokane; Tutelo; Waco; Maya; Yuci; Zapotec—names forgotten, appropriated or often ignored.

This book is guilty of starting the history of students of color in a time period long after their history began. For that, the author apologizes.

Teaching History

I had just finished teaching a university survey American History class on the Reconstruction period post the American Civil War. At the end of the lesson, an African American male student waits until everyone else has left the room and approaches exclaiming, "I am so afraid. . . ." He talks about how fearful he is as a young Black man in the southern United States and recent police shootings of unarmed Black men.

Students as well as their professors walk into classrooms full of experiences and ideas of which each know little. Much is known about the academic performance of students of color from the point of view of test results. However, not nearly enough is known from the point of view of the students. We all use formal and informal history to make sense of the present and often navigate a path between conflicting information.

The Author's Background

"The past is a foreign country." There is so much strange familiarity that assails us (Lowenthal, 1985). Growing up in the United Kingdom the author has vivid memories of her first visit to an American Airport, being handed a small red and white carton of milk. Reading the small print, "homogenized" leapt out and she refused to drink the strange word. Since then the author has visited the United States almost yearly for the past forty plus years.

In the Bronx during the 1970s the graffiti on the subways frightened her with its riot of markings and colors, and she hoped no one would see her fear. In almost the same way the words "Wogs Out" written on walls chilled her as a child in west London. But New Yorkers and Texans sensed her difference, just as she saw theirs as they rode the tube in London. And they offered her their seats on packed rides, and she has found this welcome gladdening gesture from trains in Shanghai to buses in Kathmandu. In America was learned the art of "snacking" and watching soap operas where each year the characters appeared locked in rooms or discovered long lost children or both. Conventional wisdom was learned from relatives—"there are no black men in New York, they are all in prison." Reeling from this bizarre disclosure she would when out purposely motion to someone to destroy this thesis, as if spotting some exotic flora, but quick as a flash would come the sneering retort, "nope, he is on parole." She was also privy to the sacrilege of someone daring to wear white after Labor Day, and pocketbooks not being actual books, and speaking to people and observing them look quickly behind her to see if a ventriloquist was operating a dummy. The fact that on the telephone people recognized her accent immediately, and in person children knew she was a "spice girl" but most adults could not and would not place her—that was the rule rather than the exception.

The self-conscious horror when visiting Ellis Island, of a relative looking for family among the pictures of Jewish refugees. Not too bizarre as DNA cousins later revealed. But some things were not farfetched. White flight often did mean "all the good stores have closed . . . I have to take two buses to get to my bank now . . ." The composition of neighborhoods over the past four decades changing in waves alongside the different migrant groups that made up the bulk of a city's population. Trying to understand the expression of concern as a male relative who had just started college confided "those White girls keep talking to me, but I don't want no trouble," so he refused to answer, and being reminded that a young man called "Emmett Till" may have come to his mind. And being shocked and awed at the magnificent rawness of Countee Cullen and Langston Hughes's poetry, that spoke to experiences I did not know I had, but recognized when we met on the printed page.

Holidaying is of course different from living and working in another country, which has its own challenges. However, the strangeness of living some six to eight weeks of the year, along with teaching history to American university students in the United Kingdom for ten years, and a further eleven years in the United States, shaped, and continues to shape the author, giving her ways of looking at the United States and the United Kingdom intimately. This has helped build bridges in her teaching and at times turned the author into a governess type creature, not quite family or servant in her adopted country.

Her first trip with a group of American educators underscored this. Visiting different cities, when taxis arrived they would dive into them leaving her standing bemused and a little lost. Not for them the art of "queuing" so engrained in her psyche. She has adapted, but still collides with people because she habitually walks on the "wrong" side of the corridor/hallway. She navigates through mistakes and errors, some of which she is aware of, and some which she chooses to remain oblivious of.

Learned was the trick of looking for the "flag pole or flagstaff" to find the entrance to a school building, and the agony if it is raining (the flag is removed if it is wet!) It is a good thing that many schools seem to have been designed by the same company so once you have scoped one you have your general blueprint of grade pods and spirit animals.

One aspect both countries have in common, as they share genes as historical Mother and Child is that, teaching history in the United States and the United Kingdom inevitably means at some point you are going to confront race and racism, colonies and the colonized, which from the inception of the United States, and before, and in the aftermath of the British Empire have been ingrained and controversial issues in both countries.

Collective Memory

The issue of collective memory and who and how communities of color are traditionally represented in official canons are often of paramount concern for people of color. The salience of this argument is obvious: being rooted in history seems to lend legitimacy, veneration and certainty. The awe of the ancient is, for example, often prominently observed in Asian and African societies and seems in direct opposition to habitually future-orientated Western traditions. In Western societies, the task is usually to discover, frustrate, and undermine to bring about change. By refuting accepted wisdom, Western societies seem to move on. The Darwinian tradition of survival of the fittest takes center stage. Nevertheless, the legitimacy of Western society and its justification for existence is rooted in the past (Nobles, 1992; Markus and Kitayama, 1991).

The recent past suggests that communities with histories of injustice or atrocity feel the need to remember and commemorate their collective pasts. The Truth and Reconciliation Commission in South Africa, world-wide Holocaust memorials, war memorials in the United States and war cemeteries in France are examples of communities feeling the need to remember and to commemorate. Communities may also feel the need to celebrate their triumphs more than remember their tragedies as we see in the histories of newly independent African countries in the 1960s. Therefore, they may feel the need for their history to be told not only as tragedy, but also as romance (White, 1992). They do not want to remember solely what was done to and for them, but more importantly what they did for themselves. They appear to want to be accepted and valued for who they are. The African American experience may shed further light on this, as the failure to recognize black people as human was probably a primary factor in allowing the "Peculiar Institution" and its devastating aftermath of prejudice and injustice to flourish:

> The most important legacy of the civil rights movement for black people in the Mississippi Delta is psychological: to reinstate pride in African-American history . . . the teaching of black history is essential and so neglected. Where did we fit in? We were a part of the world!". . . My own thoughts trail back to

Atlanta and the Memorial Hall quotation from Martin Luther King Jr.: "We blacks also have a soul." And the banner spread across the chest of the marcher declaring "I am a man." (Paris, 2000, p. 192)

Communities of color to some extent justify their existence by being able to answer questions asked by a person as they mature; "Who am I/Who are we?" "Where have I come from/where have we come from?" The answers come partly through a collective memory and within this concept, identification, representation, and security loom as fundamental issues. It probably is in the interest of any community wishing to promote cohesion to consciously foster and maintain a culture which values its past in terms of a collective memory. The notion of a community's collective memory often impacts on otherwise dissimilar people, and a sense of unity is nurtured which otherwise might not exist (Anderson, 1991; Penuel and Wertsch, 1998).

Because dominant groups within any given society have the power to dictate and shape national identity through an official collective memory, for marginalized groups, official collective memory usually falls short. The recurring limitations in official histories create issues of invisibility, periphery, and exclusion (Sampson, 1993). These predicaments are frequently compounded for marginal groups who often have a history of dislocation from their beginnings.

If communities are not welded together consciously through education, media. language, religion, gender or history, then they will probably either cling together because of a perceived threat or may be unable to form strong cultural identities or community collective memory. For these groups, individualistic concerns may outweigh community cohesiveness except in times of crisis. Familial and individual collective memory will probably feature more strongly for them, but the notion of a community collective memory will frequently at best be embryonic.

Identity concerns are often central to marginalized communities of color, as is the need to control their own identities and not have identities imposed on them by dominant groups. Historical representation commonly gives marginal groups recognition and a sense of legitimacy. This debate over historical representation now more than ever targets the core of cultural and national identity. When dominant groups fail to recognize the "other," it should not surprise them if such groups create their own histories which seem frequently threatening or undermining to the cohesive national identity in nation-states.

Theoretical Framework

This book probes the mental world of students of color in order to understand their perspectives on history education. As a consequence the methodological procedures sprung from the nature of the study. The history teaching background of the author also influenced how the research was approached. The methodology had to be both appropriate and practical; therefore, the theoretical framework of the book was drawn from a number of research approaches. They include Critical Race Theory, narrative analysis, hermeneutic inquiry, and aspects of historical consciousness and social constructivism and constructionist theories to explore students' interviews, surveys, and counterstories found in this work.

Critical Race Theory (CRT) originated in the late 1980s from law scholars in the United States. They examined and confronted how race and racism molded social structures of societies, their practices and discourses, by exploring and arguing for the need to listen to the lived experiences of people of color as they encountered the legal system. Derrick Bell and Alan Freeman were at the forefront of this movement, writing that critical legal studies needed to analyze race and racism for there to be real change in society. Gloria Ladson-Billings and David Gillborn have been proponents of applying CRT as a crucial theoretical framework to examine education (Taylor and et. al., 2009).

Narrative analysis is a method that gives voice to people on the margins; it helps uncover what happened or what may happen. Close to the hermeneutics approach, narrative analysis helps with interpretation and is crucial for "entering the lifeworld" of students in chapters 4, 5, 6, and 7 through their language, in interviews, surveys, and written and spoken reflections and counterstories. The narratives of students are treated as knowledge. They were systematically collected, analyzed and represent students' stories as they were told. Narrative inquiry concerns experience, and it allows us to learn. Using narrative inquiry we are "encouraged to listen to our teaching, to the stories that we, and those we teach tell" (Clandinin and Connelly, 2000. p. 17).

The work of Rüsen (1993; 2004) on the ontology of historical consciousness, with its emphasis on the temporal nature of identity, offers a valuable theoretical perspective (albeit a highly provisional one). Rüsen's suggestion of four key categories in understanding how historical consciousness operates, is a useful starting point for trying to unpack students' thinking.

Social constructivists theorize cultural differences are often crucial for understanding concepts of the inner life, such as emotions, beliefs, and attitudes. People understand themselves and others through cultural stories or through meanings and practices which are often multiple and inconsistent. Each of us sees the "real" world differently and we create our own meanings.

Social constructionists argue that individuals form their identity out of the discourses culturally available to them. Our identity forms, "not from inside the person, but from the social realm, a realm where people swim in a sea of language and other signs" (Burr, 2003, p. 109). People acquire "self as they develop language representing the structuring of experience" which has "internal logic, underlying categories, metaphors, and so on of the language we use" (Burr, 2003, p. 139). Using this theoretical basis, and research-based evidence concerning teaching and learning history, exploring psychological theories regarding aspects of learning for students of color are uncovered.

Organization of the Book

In the following chapters I report on what students of color have to say concerning their experiences with school history in the United States and the United Kingdom. I report on what they say is important for them when studying history, why they think the subject is important and why the teaching of the subject may leave them feeling apathetic and angry. I report what they thought history did on social and personal levels, and the kind of history they expected to learn. This research was carried out at the Institute of Education the University of Central London in the United Kingdom, and further research on college-aged students in the United States.

Chapters 1–3 introduce the history and contemporary context of history education in the United States and explores how students learn history including psychological theories. Chapter 4 explores the ideas of Black British students about the role and purpose of history. Chapter 5 examines a diverse group of students and their ideas about school history. Chapter 6 uncovers what American college students of color think about the history they study and the questions it raises for them. Chapters 7 and 8 detail the implications of the findings for history in education and research-based methods and strategies to better engage students of color studying history.

Acknowledgments

My thanks to all that have made this book possible. My colleagues in the History Education department, Angela De Angelo, Caroline Conner, Bryan McGovern, Chuck Wynn for their kind support and putting up with my English ways. Special thanks to Ryan Ronnenberg, who introduced me to *Baudolino*, the lying historian, and made me realize what fun team teaching could be and was instrumental in the chapter dealing with world history. Many, many thanks to Tom Okie and Tom Pusateri for their comments on early drafts, and persuading me that this was a book worth writing. My gratitude to Alice Pate, chair of the History and Philosophy Department, for her continued encouragement. Nicole Guillory's guidance and advice re urban education and on early drafts have been invaluable and I thank her for her support and cheerleading. Thank you Dr. Ann Smith who has always been in my corner with emotional, social and academic support. To Corrie Davis, and Shommari Waseme who I have never met, but they took time to read the manuscript and pointed out how this could become a better book. Thank you. To my namesake Kay Reeve and Jane McKinzey for their mentorship. To Stuart Foster and Peter Lee of the University College London (UCL) Institute of Education (IOE) University of London who took a chance on my seemly wild ideas and have been invaluable on my academic journey. My gratitude to the team at Rowman and Littlefield who have guided me through this process.

And to my friend Sonia Johnson, who has been bugging me to write a book for the past three decades, much love Son. Thank you. See! I finally took your advice. To "Win" my "skin and blister" you continue to be the "wind beneath my wings." Joy and Mauva and Aunt Zen (Norma Weir) Thank you for being there. To Tulasi Acharya, for showing me that hard work pays off, and what the words "a man's reach must exceed his grasp" truly mean.

But last and not least, my children (students), too many to name individually. You have taught me more than you will ever know. And I am eternally grateful.

CHAPTER ONE

The History of History Education for African Americans since 1800

> Until lions have their historians, tales of the hunt will always glorify the hunter.
>
> (African Proverb)

This chapter provides a brief outline of issues surrounding African American education in the United States as historical context for the rest of the book.

Antebellum Denial of African American Education

A key purpose of North American history education from the inception of the republic was to ensure that "We the People" were educated enough to understand the workings of democracy. The people, even if not full participants, were at the very least to be informed stakeholders in the "noble experiment." American democracy had always been exclusionary in terms of who "We the people" were, as gender and property qualifications had denied suffrage to women and White men without property.

During North American slavery African Americans were denied education. They were the only group for whom legislation outlawed teaching them to read and write. After the South Carolina Stono Slave Rebellion of 1739, it became a punishable offence to not only teach any enslaved person to read or write, but also to employ them to write, as educating enslaved people might endanger the system of enforced labor (Wood, 1974). But enslaved people did sometimes resist the system. For example in 1773 Phillis Wheatley, an enslaved person in Boston, Massachusetts, published "Poems on Various Subjects Religious and Moral." However, this was the exception rather than the rule. By 1800 laws against schooling for African Americans were strengthened to include the forbidding of "mental instruction," and it also became a criminal offence to teach free Black people (Williams, 2005).

Legislation also prohibited the meeting of enslaved people before or after sunset, punishable by public flogging. Such laws were aimed at clandestine schools set up by African Americans who gathered in secret to learn. African Americans opposed and circumvented such laws by holding schools in woods, by bribing White young people to teach them to read and sometimes evangelical Christianity prodded plantation owner's wives' consciences to secretly instruct enslaved people (Douglass, 1845; Jackson, 2001; Williams, 2005).

In 1808 a free Black, John Chavis, opened a school in Raleigh, North Carolina, where Whites were schooled during the day and free Blacks and enslaved people during the night. But by 1831 teaching even free Black students was forbidden by the Raleigh authorities. Other schools for African Americans such as the Charleston School for Negros was founded in South Carolina in 1810, and in the north, seven schools were opened in New York City funded by the authorities which led to free education for all Black children in New York City.

Often it seemed that the education of African Americans took one step forward and two back. For example in 1834 Oberlin College in Ohio became the first college in the west to enroll African Americans and women. However, between 1829 and 1849 Ohio prohibited African Americans from attending public schools. In 1839 Connecticut enacted a law forbidding the establishment of schools for African Americans. By the outbreak of the Civil War in 1860, Lincoln University in Pennsylvania was founded (1854), and became the first historically Black institution for tertiary education. And in 1855 Massachusetts authorities legislated against excluding individuals from public schools because of race, color or religion (Jackson, 2001). But the peculiar institution (slavery) and its racist aftermath even after its abolition, and the deadliest American war to date, tangled the very fabric of the continent.

Education Trends in the United States

On the eve of the American Civil War in 1860, 27 times more White than Black children attended schools. For the four million enslaved African Americans, illiteracy and innumeracy were the expected norms of American society. As early as 1852 calls had come from African Americans that they be allowed an education which developed their thinking and affirmed them as people who could compete with White Americans on an equal footing (Delany, 1966). However, the racist society that African Americans found themselves living in made such aspirations virtually impossible.

In 1865 the Thirteenth Amendment to the U.S. Constitution had abolished slavery and the oldest Black tertiary institution in the south, Shaw University was founded in Raleigh, North Carolina, in the same year. However, the racist education system was effective at helping to keep the status quo and this was strengthened in southern states with the enactment of "Black codes."

Black Codes
Reconstruction, the brief period after the American Civil War, saw the establishment of "Black Codes" which eventually became "Jim Crow" laws, implemented by southern governments which restricted the civil rights and liberties of the newly freed people. The post–Civil War White supremacist social structure that African Americans lived in included the policy of segregation in almost everything, such as housing, hospitals, hotels, restaurants, transportation, intermarriage, and schools. This segregated system stemmed from both historical practice and ingrained beliefs held by most White people of their superiority, by virtue of their color and the inferiority of Black people by virtue of them being Black.

Although the Fourteen and Fifteenth Amendments to the U.S. Constitution (1868 and 1870) gave Black people the right to citizenship and the right to vote, the education of African Americans seemed almost a side issue. In 1868, the Hampton Institute was founded to educate the freedmen; however, education provision was very limited, and it was church groups who chiefly worked toward educating the newly freed men and women. Eventually, African Americans established Black-run schools and universities, such as Howard in Washington, DC (named after the head of the Freedman's Bureau, the organization in charge of helping the newly freed African Americans), and Fisk University in Tennessee (Brogan, 1985).

Booker T. Washington and W.E.B. Du Bois

Education for African Americans was stunted by both legislation and practice. By 1900, the civil rights and aspirations of African Americans for education were taken up by Booker T. Washington, the head of the Tuskegee Institute in Alabama. He taught a message of circumventing racism by adopting education of a vocational nature and accepting the White supremacy social structure of the day. Washington secretly supported T. Thomas Fortune, the editor of *New York Age*, a Black newspaper which campaigned against lynching and was pro-civil rights. In his "Atlanta Compromise" speech (1895), Washington appeared to accept segregation and promoted economic advancement as a more realistic goal for African Americans.

His aspirations seemed to pander to often entrenched White views concerning African Americans, decrying Black college education for not persuading Whites that there were merits in educating Black people. Education, he argued, could improve Blacks as it had done Whites, making them productive and "useful citizens" so it was worth spending money on educating them (Washington, 1968). His colleague and eventually fiercest critic W. E. B. Du Bois disagreed with the route of waiting for White Americans to eventually grant civil rights and in 1903 put forward the concept of the "talented tenth," the idea that higher education was necessary for the leadership of the African American Community—the "talented tenth." Both education and work were essential but Black people needed the "exceptional" to lead the way to a better future.

In his book *The Souls of Black Folk*, (1903) Du Bois reasoned for immediate civil rights. His argument eventually won the day among most Black intellectuals at the time, and also historically. Historians such as Harlan and Vann Woodward (Zeringue, 2015) were divided as to Washington's legacy in terms of education. Some claimed by emphasizing industrial education Washington helped ensure African Americans were fodder for low-paying jobs. Others, however, pointed to the ingrained hostility toward African Americans' getting any education ("Educate a nigger and you spoil a good field hand" was a popular saying of the day) and for a few in the African American community, education was not always something to be proud of, as this quote from an African American biography suggests:

> George was "Deadly against Educated Niggers" and "ashamed for his children to be in school especially if they were a little more regular ahead of others." Viola held the polar view: "*How, how* could a White man [which her husband was in her view] . . . be against his child getting an Education. I thought that White . . . men and Education were Related, how could they and it be separated." (Pandey, 2013, p. 153)

In support or trying to understand Booker, T. Washington's stance, historians such as David Jackson (2008) and Robert Norrell (2011) argued that by putting such stress on vocational training Washington was circumventing White opposition to Black people getting an academic education.

At the heart of this argument concerning the kind of education best suited to African Americans lay the simple truth that most African Americans entered the American public school system from an American heritage of slavery. The school system they found themselves a part of worked well in transforming White immigrant groups into what was expected by middle-class Americans. But what did it offer people of color?

Exclusionary Stories

History was a subject that was supposed to answer questions of who Americans were as a people and suggest who they might become. But as Woodson, (1933) pointed out, African American children learned exclusionary stories of the founding of the nation. "Life, liberty and the Pursuit of Happiness did not include them. Stories of the American Revolution and the struggle to be free did not include them. They were taught the values of White society and appropriate middle-class behavior, but they also learned by default that they were invisible. The idea of universal education founded on equality, equity and quality, did not differentiate in terms of its diverse population. Reasons for this stemmed from a variety of hegemonic beliefs and theories, from the supposed biblical curse of being sons of Ham (who had sinned against their father Noah and were doomed in perpetuity as servants), to scientific 'discoveries.'"

Between 1870 and 1900, civilizing missions in Europe and North America became the norm based on ideas of Western moral and racial superiority. Pseudo-science such as Phrenology, the use of skull shape to determine a person's place in a "hierarchy of races" flourished. Such "science" was said to prove the biological inferiority of non-Whites who were little more than children or animals in need of taming (Fallace, 2012). Western culture was habitually seen as the pinnacle of human development. All other groups were commonly inferior, deficient and problematic, in short "the White Man's Burden." The British poet Kipling, an avowed racist, penned his poem "The White Man's Burden" concerning the American invasion of the Philippines as defense for the Imperialism enveloping Europe as it practiced the three Cs of Colonization: "Civilization, Christianity and Commerce."

In the United States, the ascribed inferiority of Black people manifested itself in expected acts of deference toward White people in a multitude of ways, such as using back doors when entering their homes. Whites overwhelmingly had the power to do as they pleased with the civil rights of people of color because they held the reigns of both private and public power. White supremacy was prominently displayed in 1896 when the Supreme Court in the *Plessy v. Ferguson* decision upheld racist southern legislation by adopting the principle of "separate but equal." The ruling asserted state governments were fulfilling their responsibilities to their African American citizens if they had "separate but equal" facilities.

Although a major setback to the African American community, Black people continued planning and establishing places of education such as the

American Negro Academy for African American arts and sciences founded (1897) in Washington D.C., by Alexander Crummel. Forums to fight for political, economic, social and educational equality, such as the National Association for the Advancement of Colored People (NAACP) established in 1909 as an integrated organization, grew in prestige in the Black community (Jackson, 2001).

History Education
The end of the American Civil War saw a wide-scale rewriting of American history by southerners. Historians and political scientists such as W. A. Dunning (1907) gave lie to the claim that "victors write history." In his book "Reconstruction, Political and Economic, 1865–1877," Dunning, portrayed Reconstruction as an era of cruel oppression, when the Former Confederate States had been tortured and ruled by tyrannical zealots. Slavery had been benevolent, and indeed the Civil War had been caused by fanatics such as John Brown and the Abolitionists, who fought to get rid of a system that would have died naturally.

Giving citizenship to African Americans was a mistake as Whites would never accept them as equals. Southern heroes were President Andrew Jackson, the southern Redeemers and White terrorist organizations such as the Ku Klux Klan. This was the generally accepted version of this portion of American history that filtered into school history until the mid-twentieth century, and gave "scientific" grist for the continuation of segregation and the widespread belief in the inferiority of African Americans (Woodson, 1933).

In the early twentieth century, school history was a dominant subsection of social education including geography and civics. History's role was to develop a sense of patriotism, inculcate societal values and teach students how to be good citizens of the Republic. Popular discriminatory notions concerning people of color unsurprisingly filtered into the history curriculum.

This undoubtedly inculcated and fostered a sense of superiority in White students. Racist theories concerning race and theories of Social Darwinism created and maintained notions of White supremacy that found their way into progressive pedagogy. History was the main vehicle transporting societal values; therefore, it played a dominant role in fostering racial attitudes toward "others" (Nelson and Pang, 2014; Fallace, 2012). To circumvent some of these ideas Carter G. Woodson began the Association for the Study of Negro Life and History in 1915 and called for the establishment of a Black History Week (Jackson, 2001).

Despite being treated as second-class citizens African Americans joined the armed forces during the Great War, 1914–1918, most serving in labor battalions performing menial but crucial tasks. Returning from the war they looked for a better life, including more educational opportunities. The end of the Great War promoted the exodus of between 450,000 to 500,000 African Americans from southern states to the North, and in the 1920s, the Great Migration as it was called saw a further 700,000 Black southerners move north (Arnesen, 2003).

Marcus Garvey and Black Consciousness

In 1916 the histories of the Caribbean African diaspora and African Americans continued to intertwine with the arrival of Marcus Garvey from Jamaica. He forcefully campaigned for Black people to love themselves and be proud of their African heritage, a message woefully missing in the lives of many in the African American community (Grant, 2008). As Woodson in 1933, James in 1954, Malcom X in 1964, Bullock in 1967, Hale-Benson in 1986, Asante in 1991, and many others since, have noted, American history, almost always excluded people of color from the dominant narrative as people with any agency.

The caste system of skin color present in the Caribbean was also alive and well in the United States, another relic of slavery. Being able to pass the brown paper bag test was still a reality, and many lighter skinned African Americans were not drawn to Garvey's "Back to Africa" movement, leaving it fragmented. But others were drawn, including Claude McKay, another West Indian, whose sonnet "If we must die" captured the hope, fear and resilience of the African American community. By 1925, half a million urban African Americans had joined Garvey's Universal Negro Improvement Association, despite his incarceration in 1923 when he was conveniently convicted of mail fraud, subsequently jailed, and deported to Jamaica in 1927 (Grant, 2008).

However, once something has been heard, it cannot be unheard and the continued awakening of Black consciousness remained in the hearts and minds of many African Americans and people of the Caribbean. Continuing to highlight deficiencies in education in 1932, Howard University started "The Journal of Negro Education" which published research pertaining to issues and challenges facing African Americans. The United Negro College Fund, a consortium of thirty-nine Historically Black Colleges and Universities (HBCUs) was founded in 1944. Their aim was to enhance higher education for African American students by providing them with scholarships and raising funds, and supplying assistance to member institutions. The growing civil rights movement was becoming pivotal in ushering in demands for change in American life—economic, political, social and educational—which were not fully appreciated until the middle of the century (Grant, 2008).

Carter G. Woodson
The publication in 1933 of Carter G. Woodson's study on African American education was seminal in pointing out the many ways in which the education system often damaged the African American community. His calls for a Black History week would eventually become Black History Month.

Woodson's appeals for reform were taken up in the 1940s by American civil rights activists who agitated for an end to segregation in education; they demanded more representation of people of color at all levels of the education system along with curriculum reform. In the public-school system demands continued for the revision of teaching and instructional materials, and how schools were funded. Black activists also began to insist school boards be representative of the school populations they served in terms of diversity (Weinberg 1991). But by the 1950s "seventy-five million dollars of public funds each year went to Southern educational institutions that do not admit African Americans" (Jackson, 2001, P.52).

Education Since the *Brown v. Board of Education Topeka* Decision

Brown v. Board of Education, Topeka, Kansas (1954), eventually overturned the separate but equal fallacy of *Plessy v. Ferguson* with the Supreme Court's decision that separate educational facilities were psychologically damaging to Black children even if they were equal, which of course they seldom were.

From one perspective the Brown decision is a seminal piece of legislation in the Civil Rights movement for African Americans. Another perspective is that the ruling had more to do with Cold War rhetoric and protecting the United States from outside criticism than actual reform (Dudziak, 2009). Although the reasons behind the ruling have blurred over time, the fact that Brown galvanized White segregationists is not in dispute. In the Deep South states, of Alabama, Georgia, South Carolina, Louisiana, and Mississippi, Whites preferred to see their schools close rather than integrate.

Most southern politicians signed the Southern Manifesto which committed them to fight against the Brown decision and defied any interference from the federal government. President Eisenhower, not a supporter of Brown, was eventually forced to act when a school in Little Rock, Arkansas, became a flashpoint. In 1957, Central High School caught worldwide attention when the then Governor Orval Faubus, up for reelection, decided to gain support for his reappointment campaign by hitching it to the wagon of anti-integration supporters.

In September 1957, Faubus ordered the Arkansas National Guard to Central High to prevent African American students from entering the school.

The decision of President Eisenhower to send in federal troops was not a show of support for integration, but rather, he cautioned, to enforce law and order on "disorderly mobs." The world looked on at the spectacle of nine Black children forced to run the gamut of an abuse-hurling mob at Central High School, and many wondered how the United States could criticize the South African government for their policy of apartheid (Dentler, 1991).

Sputnik and Education
When the Soviet Union launched the first satellite, Sputnik, in 1957 amid the Cold War it provoked widespread questioning of North American education, and the demand to prepare American students for a new technological future, with a focus on Science and Technology. The federal government responded with the National Defense Education Act (1958), sponsoring and financing innovations in education, including the teaching of social studies deemed crucial for national defense. Social studies programs such as Edwin Fenton's and John Good's "New Social Studies" and Paul Hannah's "Expanding Horizons" curriculum were organized around social science concepts and processes.

However, the snail's pace of integration meant, by 1962, only 2 percent of African American students in the southern states of Alabama and South Carolina attended integrated schools. Sixty plus years after Brown, schools with majority students of color are frequently still woefully underfunded in terms of money, school buildings, educators, and the curriculum.

Deficit Cultures

In Frank Riessman's book *The Culturally Deprived Child* (1962), written about the assets of children deemed by middle-class society as "culturally deprived," he pointed out that while some working-class children might be deficient in the mores and values of the middle class, they had their own culture with their own assets. Considering this, schools should make the most of the nonverbal learning styles of such children. He stressed schools should not try to turn these students into acceptable replicas of an alien class. Critics cautioned that being nonverbal was probably not going to make children in the already middle-class school system academically successful. Plus, the idea that certain verbal skills were deemed "middle class" ruffled academic feathers.

Black social scientist Kenneth Clark (1971) attacked the "cult of cultural deprivation" being used to explain the underperformance of Black children at school. He chided that to say cultural deprivation was the cause was as deterministic as using the defective genes theory as an explanation for poor academic performance. The excuse of cultural deprivation for academic underperformance could allow biased teachers to claim children were unable to learn because of their defective backgrounds.

Clark cautioned children were not learning because they were not being taught. Their teachers did not believe they could learn, and they lived up to their teacher's expectations. For others the issue was one of teachers being out of their depth when it came to schooling lower-income Black students and students of the working class. This is still in the twenty-first century said to be an issue.

The pressing concern for African Americans in the 1960s was integration and civil rights. With the assassination of President Kennedy in 1963, his successor, a consummate politician, Lyndon B. Johnson pushed a civil rights act through the House and Senate to become law in 1964 in a grieving nation. The Civil Rights Act of 1964 outlawed segregation in public places and directed that color not be used as a reason to deny civil rights, and color blindness was to end racial intolerance and prejudice.

In 1965, riots broke out in the Watts district of Los Angeles, and, in the following two years, similar disturbances occurred in largely Black neighborhoods. The controversial American Moynihan Report, released in 1965, turned the attention of the American public to theories of cultural deprivation in families of people of color with its claim that "at the heart of the deterioration of the fabric of Negro society is the deterioration of the Negro family (Moynihan 1965)."

Title 1 and Head Start
In 1965, President Johnson turned his focus to poverty and providing better schools for impoverished children, many of whom happened to be children of color. The purpose of Head Start was to prepare children whose family income was below the poverty line to be better prepared for school. It was designed to provide intellectual, social and emotional welfare for such students. The involvement of parents and the wider community was seen as pivotal.

Johnson's Elementary and Secondary Education Act (ESEA) allocated federal money based on the number of poor students in schools. The Title 1 program of ESEA was widely welcomed because every district in America received Title 1 federal funding.

In the 1970s, ESEA was expanded to include funds for bilingual and Native American education, drug education, and school lunch and breakfast programs. The aims of the program were never clearly defined and have come under criticism. The program's unclear contours of not only improving education but also aspects of social work, libraries, nutrition and medical services added to a lack of clarity in the eyes of detractors.

Conservative critics like Ravitch (1983) pointed out that there was scant evidence to show that Title 1 was effective at closing the gap between the academic achievements of poor children in comparison with their middle-class counterparts. She claimed those running and those evaluating the program had diverging goals. In 1999 an attempt was made by President Clinton to reauthorize ESEA, but it was not passed by both houses of Congress in 2000 (Jackson, 2001).

The Coleman Report (1966)

The Coleman Report on American education produced findings that for many were troubling:

Most American schools were mono racial.
White Schools had some benefits in terms of material assets over Black schools; however, "American schools were virtually separate and equal."
Students of color trailed academically some three to five years behind their White counterparts at twelfth grade.
Academic Achievement seemed to correlate to family background—not inferiority or excellence of school.
The collective composition of the school and the students' perception of the situation was related to academic achievement.

The reaction of the American public to the report was generally schools don't make a difference, and therefore improving schools was unlikely to have much effect on student achievement. This raised doubts about compensatory education that had been sold as a panacea to close the achievement gap of poor students (Jackson, 2001).

Students Taking Center Stage

By 1968, the assassination of Martin Luther King added fuel to already inflamed feelings of injustice felt by African Americans. Rioting in several major cities erupted. The quagmire of the Vietnam War pulled President Lyndon Johnson deeper than he wanted to go, and serious civil unrest at home made for a volatile presidency. And in the early 1970s the Civil Rights Movement and the morality of the Vietnam War shifted the focal point of educators concerning the role and purpose of education away from the dominant role of the teacher. Students now took center stage. Paulo Freire's *Pedagogy of the Oppressed* (1968) was key in this movement as was Benson's Snyder's *The Hidden Curriculum* (1971).

During the 1970s and 1980s social scientists continued to make connections between race, class and learning. The variety of euphemisms were often only thinly veiled descriptions of Black students. This genetic speculation gained a new lease on life with the publication of Herrnstein and Murray's

The Bell Curve (1994), and the continuing debate about issues of diversity and inclusion like Affirmative Action rumble on unabated to the present day.

Busing and Integration

In 1971 the Supreme Court ruled the desegregation of schools should be fully implemented in the *Swann v. Mecklenburg* decision. For this to be done some White children were transported (bused) long distances to attend schools with African American populations to ensure integration. President Nixon was like many Whites against the practice of busing and funded White only schools. Furthermore, he helped retard integration with his appointment of four conservative judges to the Supreme Court which secured a victory against the practice of busing in the *Milliken v. Bradley* (1974) ruling which basically reintroduced segregation in schools via the back door.

A plethora of acts from the late 1960s to the present day have characterized changes in education and have significantly impacted students of color.

Legislation

Bilingual Education Act (1968–2001)
The changing demographics of the United States engendered the Bilingual Education Act (1968–2001) when Congress authorized relevant instruction funds in response to the rise in numbers of students for whom English was an additional language.

Title IX (1972)
This regulation prohibited discrimination based on sex. A comprehensive law, it protected the rights of both males and females from preschool through graduate school in sports, financial aid, employment, counseling, school regulations, and policies, admissions, and other areas.

PL 94–142 (1975) Later Became Individuals with Disabilities Education Act (1991, 1997)
This act provided financial assistance to local school districts to provide free and appropriate education for children with disabilities who were between the ages of 3 and 21.

A Nation at Risk (1983)
In 1983 the National Commission on Educational Excellence published a damming report that claimed United States public schools were failing their students. Schools were characterized by mediocrity. The inadequate rigor of

United States education had put the nation at risk, losing ground to other nations in commerce, industry, science, and technology. The commission believed fewer electives, and greater emphasis on academic subjects was necessary to begin to rectify this threat. Responses to this report included teacher and student accountability measures through testing and curricular revisions with more emphasis on standard content.

No Child Left Behind Act (2001)

This act called for increasing accountability for states in the form of standards: for school districts and for schools with annual testing of math and reading in grades 3-8 and at least once during high school. The law codified the principles of Outcome Based Education. States were prompted to adopt performance based tests and Adequate Yearly Progress provisions. These were determined by the state. A key aim was the closing of the achievement gap between low-income students, special education students, and racial minorities. All students had to reach proficiency by the 2013–2014 school year. If students did not meet Adequate Yearly Progress the schools could not receive additional funds and they could be closed. Teachers could also be removed.

The power of this AYP-or-else mandate should not be underestimated as the Atlanta Public Schools cheating scandal in Georgia demonstrated. In 2009 educators were accused of changing students' answers on state-administered standardized tests and the subsequent trial 2014–2015 demonstrated the influence of testing on educator accountability and the repercussions.

NCLB gave parents greater freedom to select schools, with increased federal support for charter schools. It promoted increased emphasis on literacy and mandated that supplemental educational services be offered. Implementing new curriculum, appointing experts to advise schools, extending the length of the school day or year and changing a school's internal organization were all part of its remit.

By the end of the 2005–06 school year, all teachers were to be "highly qualified." New teachers had to be holders of at least a bachelor's degree. Elementary school teachers had to pass state tests demonstrating their subject knowledge and teaching skills. Middle and high school teachers needed to be either university graduates, or had completed coursework equivalent to an undergraduate university degree. By the end of the 2007–08 school year, testing was to be conducted in science once during grades 3–5, 6–9, and 10–12.

NCLB was criticized for several reasons including not supporting early learning. The chief issue, however, was that initiatives such as remedial programs were not funded. The system of punishments in place for failing AYP in some quarters led to lower expectations being set to mitigate and cushion against possible punishment. Furthermore, the arts, social studies and language arts instructional time was reduced. ESL (English as a Second Language) students had a three-year time period to take assessments in their native language, but only ten states did this.

In-Service and Pre-Service Teachers

Although much has changed, many things remain the same. In the twenty-first century we find young American teachers and pre-service teachers growing up in the late 1990s and early 2000s in a seemingly diverse world. However, de facto segregation still exists in many areas of the United States. Therefore, it comes as no surprise that explorers of university life find students generally mix with people they grew up with and have relatively few friends or acquaintances from different cultures (Nathan, 2006).

The systematic racist legacy of the American past means students and teachers sometimes unknowingly grapple with the often unnoticed, silent, vivid, lived, racist experiences, of non-White students. Some of these students are being taught in White educational spaces. Consequently, as educators the need arises to be proactive and challenge their own and that of their students' personal beliefs and invisible values along with attitudes to enable more equitable teaching and learning (Rubie-Davis, 2007).

Approaches and strategies in teacher preparation courses often tackle issues like race and class separately from discrete disciplines such as history and pedagogical knowledge, or courses may claim to "infuse" such issues. Also, frequently instruction on pedagogical differentiation and scaffolding is commonly handled as if they are discrete entities which may make for a peppered, rather than targeted approach. There is often a failure to link them securely to individual disciplines.

That said, over time more awareness has arisen concerning the way cultures and students' backgrounds affect views of lesson content and classroom experiences. But frequently, teachers mention a lack of resources, knowledge and the skills to equitably serve the needs of students of color they encounter and teaching such knowledge, it is regularly argued, lies beyond comfort zones. Most of North America's future teachers are White, female and middle-class, and increasingly many of the students they will teach are not, undoubtedly making for a cultural mismatch between students and teachers (Neal, and et al, 2003; El-Haj, 2006; Feistritzer, 2011).

In 2019 the National Council for the Social Studies (NCSS) joined with seventy-five education groups to support a call for increased diversity among teacher candidates, quoting federal and university data that in the public school system only 18 percent of teachers identify as people of color, while the public school students they teach are 53 percent students of color (Association of American Educators Foundation 2019 aaeteachers.org/diversity).

Fifty-seven percent of history/social studies teachers in the American school system are male "coaches" teaching a variety of sports with social studies (School and Staffing Survey, 2011).[1] Teaching social studies for some is secondary to coaching and has much more appeal in the workplace. Many schools in the United States are also seriously engaged in stemming hemorrhaging high school drop-out rates of designated students of color. And the revolving doors of the school to prison pipeline are well documented. Moreover, in 2014, (the latest data at the time of writing), history was the subject African Americans did most poorly at in terms of proficiency (National Assessment of Educational Progress, 2014).

In 2014 more bachelor of history degrees were awarded to Hispanics, rising from 4.4 percent in 1995 to 9.6 percent in 2014. But, the 5 percent of African Americans awarded bachelor's degrees in history was basically the same as they were in 1995 when records began (National Center for Education Statistics, 2018).

Considering all the subjects on the curriculum, why do African Americans find history so difficult or not worth studying? This is the question history educators and those that write history or decide on history curricula, national or state, should be asking, but most are not. On the cusp of a new decade the world is becoming more divided on matters of race, inclusion and equality, and the silence of educators equals complicity.

American Schools in the Twenty-First Century

Teaching in the United States, one is quickly confronted with the term "Urban Schools," which is much like the British phrase "Inner City Schools," both being shorthand for schools with a high proportion of non-White children and often places with underachieving students. Urban schools in the United States when compared to their suburban counterparts are commonly underfunded, have issues of low graduation rates, high teacher turnover and problems with violence coupled with disciplinary disproportionality. Social scientists still make connections between race, class and learning and a variety of euphemisms are regularly veiled descriptions of African American students (Kozol, 1992; Lewis and et al., 2012). In 2018 an African American student in one of the author's classes wrote:

> *Plessy v. Fergusson*: . . . This courtcase established the doctrine of "separate but equal" which was obviously not true because although the schools were indeed separate, they weren't equal at all in treatment or educationally. Imagine

already being behind from being in the south, but also being held down more because of your skin color. Another thing that is still in play now. Although we may have more "freedom of choice" of where we go to school, a lot of schools in Black communities are of course predominately African American but also still run down, teachers do not care, we still have a lack of knowledge on our own history, the supplies are trashy . . . the list goes on.

As he wrote the country was again embroiled in racial controversy concerning Black athletes "taking the knee" during the playing of the National Anthem to protest police slayings of unarmed mostly young black men. The vitriol these people received on social media is indicative of the hostile racial politics enveloping the country since the 2016 presidential election.

In 1903 W.E.B. Dubois stated the problem of the twentieth century in the United States was the problem of the color line. In 1944 Gunnar Myrdal's book "American Dilemma" painted a bleak picture of the African American experience. More than a century later color prejudice is, despite the passing of time and laws, still very much an issue for people of color, and those supposedly without color (Bonilla-Silva, 2010).

Educators need to ask themselves a question: What is the goal of history education? Is it to promote social cohesiveness in communities by seemingly teaching students to suppress and subordinate personal cultural roots and the similarities they have with the rest of the world, instead focusing on the uniqueness of their "imagined community" the "exceptional nation"? Or, conversely, is history teaching at its best when it is fostering the idea of global connections and the interdependence of people? Or can history in education do both?

Note

1. The field of high school social studies attracts more men than women. This goes against the general trend of preservice teaching education. One widely accepted anecdotal explanation is the strong draw of coaching sports in high schools. Schools expect and advertise their social studies openings as including the ability to coach a sport, thus it is a well-worn route to employment.

CHAPTER TWO

How Students Learn History and Why It Matters

> Janie saw her life like a great tree in leaf with the things suffered, things enjoyed, things done and undone. Dawn and doom was in the branches.
>
> (Huston, 1937)

In this chapter how students learn history and the significance of this for teaching history to students of color is discussed along with the importance of alternative narratives including Afrocentric and multicultural narratives.

Why How Students Learn History Is Important

In the mid-1990s along with changes in the content of history lessons, more research emphasis in history education was given to the "nature of history" as a form of knowledge and to the way students learn. The belief that history teachers needed to give more importance to structural understandings and second-order concepts in the ideas of students as they learned history grew. If teachers do not know the ideas students held re the nature of history or develop a more informed understanding of the way students learning history understood structural concepts, they "cannot address them, and much of the substance of history will be distorted and constrained by children's tacit assumptions" (Lee, 1995, p. 95).

Research into the kinds of knowledge that teachers communicated directly or indirectly to their students demonstrated that teachers were not passive transmitters of knowledge. Educators' prior experiences, beliefs, attitudes and ways of looking at the world shaped teaching and therefore, indirectly or directly, affected those taught and probably how and what was taught. The same was true of students assimilating history.

Studies pointed out learning history was not just a neutral academic endeavor. Much of what was learned as history was socially constructed and not just impartial academic information. Increasingly history was recognized as a discipline that was assimilated through communal customs and internal beliefs. Individuals accumulated copious amounts of information from a variety of sources in order to make sense of the world. This information was then sifted and analyzed using the tools of present-day thinking which were strongly influenced by socio-cultural heritage and the dominant attitudes present in a society's historical consciousness.

Understanding Students' Thinking about History: Why Inclusive Narratives Are Important

Is it important to understand how students use the history they know to cope with present-day problems? If so, why? From research by Wertsch (1994) you gain clues as to why the cultural tools of collective historical narratives commonly "empower" or "constrain action." Using the example of American students who could not write a historical narrative from the viewpoint of a non-White group utilizing American history, students were unable to produce a historical narrative that was inclusive of multicultural histories within American society. What was striking was that they expressed some form of unease with the "story-line" they adopted to complete the assignment.

The students had only learned a single way of looking at their society's history, a dominant narrative that stifled other options and voices. They did not have sophisticated "cultural tools" and the cultural tools that they were using had an "integrated and exclusionary structure that made it difficult for other voices to participate" (Wertsch, 1994, p. 336). The students could not use what they had not been given and were unable to voice any other story apart from the dominant cultural narrative of their society. The way students are regularly socialized and taught impacts on their ability to function with alternative historical narratives.

This research is decades old, but its implications are fundamental for history educators serious about correcting inequalities within history education. If school history fails to give students alternative cultural tools, students will habitually find it difficult to function effectively in diverse environments.

Teaching and Learning History

Researchers like Levstik (2000) shed further light on what students, teachers and preservice teachers see as important when learning and teaching history. People develop alternative histories through a variety of means within society ranging from cultural norms and religions they practice to museums visited and media, conventional and social. Therefore, they must often navigate through a minefield of varying accounts and somehow try to reconcile the anomalies encountered.

For this reason, students of color frequently have challenges reconciling their own notions about history they learn outside the classroom, with the history they encounter in history lessons. This commonly becomes problematical, because they learn a dominant storyline which at times is difficult to reconcile with their lived experiences and history, learned from alternative sources outside of their schooling. In short, the complicated nature of American history is often ignored in school history classes to the detriment of all students.

This neglect frequently damages students because they do not have a framework with which they can begin to conceptualize their own lives in a historical context. Without this grounding, frequently students cannot fully understand the inequalities and injustices in their own and other societies. "Instead they are faced with a history long on myth, short on intellectual rigor, and extraordinarily slow to incorporate the wide range of behavior that has characterized American history" (Levstik, 2000, p. 290).

Interestingly, some interviewees in Levstik's study were aware of anomalies between the history they learned in school, their lived lives, and history learned from other sources. For example, African American students were familiar with the continuation of racism within American society. They found narratives suggesting America was a free and equal culture difficult to reconcile and understand in the light of what they knew about prejudice, such as the treatment of recent immigrants to the United States. Both African American students and White students tended to see the past as useful in terms of learning from its mistakes but, African American students used a more thorny evaluation of the route America took to extend civil rights to marginalized groups.

African American students also spoke concerning the absence of "civil rights" history in their schools; they reported that they learned about such issues at home and watching films but that the topic was largely absent from school history. Tellingly, Levstik further observed that at times during her interviews students fell silent. She gives the example of a White American student who argued "we're all equal now" and the silence of an African American student who only rejoined the conversation when it shifted to inequalities concerning Native Americans.

Levstik's work yields other complex results. Teachers and preservice teachers spent much less time discussing the issue of the continuation of racism within American society than students. They talked a lot about "inclusion." Discussions of "racism" and "ethnicity" were subsumed and embraced under the "issue of culture." In other words, teachers acted as "gatekeepers" on potentially controversial issues rather than "gate openers" on matters of racism and ethnicity. Talk about issues of racism and discrimination was also more likely to arise from students in schools with an ethnically diverse population. Likewise, teachers in ethnically diverse settings were more likely to tackle "race" issues.

Moreover, frequently the students were interested "in exactly the areas that teachers and teacher candidates found profoundly disturbing" (Levstik, 2000, p. 296). In the author's experience of classroom interactions this is too often the case. Observing a middle school lesson on NAFTA (North American Free Trade Agreement), which had recently been the subject of much media coverage because of President Trump's moves to renegotiate the treaty terms, a student of Mexican heritage wanted to talk about the Mexican issues in the media concerning the treaty widely expressed by the president. One word, "political," from the teacher was used to silence him.

It was a clear signal in the classroom for students to desist and stay clear of a controversial topic. Teachers are frequently aware of the dichotomy of their wanting to produce a national history that is "beneficent" and students wanting to understand more about histories and the present that did not fit neatly into this sanitized mold. In their defense teachers and pre-service teachers argued that they had not been equipped to understand history in "sophisticated ways," nor had they been taught how to understand and explore the complex nature of American history when they were learning history.

Teachers knew that there were anomalies, but they often wanted to skim over these and create a "common identity"; doing otherwise would be opening Pandora's box. Therefore, the teachers "chose silence," the easy or less scenic route. In choosing to remain silent and tackling only safe issues like "salsa, and soul food," teachers are habitually unintentionally offering the students they teach distortions of history and the present day. When educators fail to engage fully or fairly with the histories of multicultural students it should not surprise them that these students end up rejecting such history as false and irrelevant.

History teachers need to help students build a framework from which they can make sense of the complexities of alternative histories that they may hear outside of the classroom and from significant others. Without such a framework, students may choose alternative routes that clash with the dominant narrative or become cynical or apathetic.

These observations about possible reasons for the alienation and non-involvement of students of color in the history classroom are not new, but regularly go largely unnoticed. They have decisive implications for history teachers who should want to enhance their understanding and not ignore how students move between what they teach and what students perceive as social realities.

The significance of the concept of "inclusion" being used as a cover that avoids, rather than tackles, sensitive issues should be a wake-up call or at the very least set alarm bells ringing. It is reminiscent of the view that multicultural education in the United Kingdom is often superficial "saris, samosas and steel-bands." In trying to be even-handed or "color-blind" teachers may negate or affirm histories of multicultural groups in unintended and undesirable ways.

How Students Make Sense of History

How do students make sense of all the images they learn about the past? If assessments are often only telling us what students don't know and not what they "do know," educators are regularly at a disadvantage. How can history be taught more effectively if there is ignorance concerning the way young people form and use their historical context? Advances in understanding how the learning process works means much more is known concerning how students' beliefs and ideas often shape what they take from instruction (Wineburg, 2000).

Nevertheless, history as a discipline lags behind subjects like mathematics that have revamped textbooks to address the "misconceptions" and faulty notions children bring when learning different aspects of the subject. History topics have changed and become more inclusive of some multicultural groups, but not enough is known about the way students studying history use their thinking about the subject. Textbooks are likely to work on the premise that students have no prior knowledge of history. This is far from the truth as by the time students reach adolescence, they have encountered histories in multiple grades and been bombarded with alternative histories from a variety of sources, beginning at home. History educators must be more aware of the challenges arising in the minds of students as they attempt to reconcile clashing histories they encounter in and outside of formal history education.

Other studies such as Wineburg (2000) give a more comprehensive understanding of how "social beliefs converge in people's thinking about the past" (p. 311). Interviewing fifteen students and their parents, he wanted to explore differences between "lived memory and learned memory" (p. 313). He found that "historical memory" appears "highly selective" and people's recollections are "constantly being shaped by the contemporary social processes" such as books, films and social needs that resurrect some issues from the past and not others (pp. 321–322). Ultimately, Wineburg reasons understanding in some small part "how adolescents make sense of the past, we can learn how to better engage their historical beliefs, stretch them, and call them into question when necessary" (p. 322).

Much necessary work has gone into students' understandings of second order concepts such as evidence and explanation in history (Lee, 1995). But, many of the presumptions, expectations and misconceptions that students, especially different cultural groups, use are mostly still to a great extent unidentified.

African Americans and History Lessons

Research by Epstein (1997) uncovers some of this vagueness. Studying students in an inner city Midwestern school, over the long run she found that African American children and White American students taking the same classes had different perspectives about what they had learned about American history. African American students in fact picked out individuals and events related to African American freedom as the most significant areas of study, and White American students' perceptions were that people and events concerning the development of the United States were most important.

Why this difference? Epstein suggests the reason for this marked variance is the White American students' saw the rights of the individual and society as an "unalienable characteristic" of the story of America. African American students, however, saw a "contradiction" between the ideal of "citizenship" and the reality of the denial of rights to African Americans and other multicultural groups within American society. Epstein concluded African American students also gave more credence to historical knowledge from family members than from their teachers or their textbooks.

This was in direct contrast to White students who believed the opposite. African American students additionally thought African American teachers had more "access to accurate information on African American history" (Ibid., p. 29). In other words, marginal groups may hold their own unofficial histories in higher regard than they do official accounts. Epstein writes African American students used the coping mechanism of a "double historical consciousness," one that reflected the official history of America learned from teachers and textbooks, and the other that reflected the unofficial history they constructed from family and other sources. Further,

> Pedagogical reforms aimed solely at the development of conceptual thinking do not address the problems that arise when school based historical knowledge and perspectives differ from those that young people from ethnically or culturally diverse communities have constructed from family members and from other sources. . . . Social and cultural contexts . . . influence children's and adolescents' historical understanding. (p. 31)

In earlier work, Epstein (1993, p. 281) focused on the notion that students needed to be made aware that issues such as "race, ethnicity, gender or class lead to multiple and often conflicting perspectives in and on historical texts." Also, students should be taught that it is necessary to be aware of their "ability to recognize the relationship between the historian's perspective and his or her shaping of the historical narrative." Epstein's argument is that "factors like race, ethnicity and social class may shape young people's historical thought and how classroom interactions among the teacher, texts and students affect young people's abilities and willingness to learn history" (1997, p. 31).

The key point of this research is the minds of students are often made malleable by a variety of sources and some of these influences are more important than others.

Afrocentric Narratives

One way to look at calls for Afrocentric history is to understand it as growing out of the continued concern about Black civil rights in the 1960s. This led to more frequent calls for framers of school curricula to acknowledge the diverse and complex nature of national society in the United States. The history of history education demonstrated the absence of people of color from American history. If you are absent from history you do not exist.

Legislation from colonial times prevented Black people getting an education. When African Americans became consumers of public education it was as invisible people in a story where they were largely unacknowledged. Black students could study American History and not learn anything about themselves. The idea of Afro-centric narratives and Black studies was to right some of these wrongs. These resulted in programs of study aimed mainly at Black experience with mixed results.

Lee and Slaughter-Defoe (2003) in the Handbook of research on Multicultural Education defined Afro-centricity as "the African experience as a shared orientation among peoples of African descent both on the continent of Africa and throughout the Diaspora, based on similar cultural, historical, and political experiences" (p.356). The Afro-centric position implied Western academic learning was an alien culture.

Theories regarding what students viewed as "acting White" or taking on "White" characteristics surfaced as being an effort by some students of color to defy the position they were assigned in society, by rejecting majoritarian values and behavior in the classroom (Ogbu, 1995). Recently, Emdin (2016) underscores the necessity of new approaches and "Reality Pedagogy" when teaching students of color in urban settings who do not respond to traditional pedagogy.

Writers from an Afro-centric position stressed that to meet the needs of children of the African diaspora, educators must recognize and value their cultural and racial identities. Key is the inclusion of African history in the classroom. This they argued would bolster the self-esteem of Black children; making it easier for them to take up academic subjects without losing self-respect and identity, which they claimed was one of the results of sometimes traumatizing Eurocentric curricula.

Accordingly, when history pertaining to Africa and the African diaspora was rewritten from a Eurocentric position to an Afro-centric position, it repaired the negative image of African peoples that children of African descent had traditionally experienced. Euro-American philosophies differed from African philosophy; consequently when African data were processed using European principles the finished product was distorted. The European world-views' guiding principle was survival of the fittest and control over nature, which affected the character of European values and customs. African philosophy was community orientated rather than individual concentrated (Nobles, 1992).

The call was made for the inclusion in the educational system of an African philosophy of life (King, and Swartz, 2019). History as taught in schools was exclusionary. People of the African diaspora suffered more than any other group because of the distortion or erasure of their histories. History also preserved nineteenth-century racist deficit agendas and doctrines that went unchallenged within the school curriculum. The image of Africa and Africans presented to students was one of base humanity. Afro-centric history would give those with African roots and White students a new perspective of things African. This in turn would enable Black children to begin to close the academic gap. Of course, this placed enormous emphasis on the influence of school history.

The whole notion was plausible but for some too simplistic as it ignored a plethora of other challenges facing students of color, and their schooling in the American educational system. The call for Black history or studies was not new. Black studies was recognized as a discipline. In the United States universities offer courses on it, but was not a magic bullet. Even in the early 1980s critics claimed that Black studies circumvented the opportunities of those that chose to take it as the major focus of their degrees, "the graduate in Black Studies is equipped for only a very limited role in a multiracial society, his qualification is of value only in areas of employment while Black Studies has validity (Lincoln quoted in Edgington, 1982)."

Nevertheless, Black studies gave life to the experiences of the Black community, and explained the realities they faced with White people and suggested why they faced them. It explained the big picture, why there were haves and have-nots, why the Black experience had often been marked as one of struggle, a struggle which was very different than that of most White Americans.

Multiculturalism

The collective memory of early American society as a cacophony of difference in terms of people and languages has been largely and perhaps conveniently forgotten. Second and third generation children of color frequently are labeled different and not belonging by virtue of these differences. Therefore, they are often forced to demonstrate their assimilation. For people of color to assimilate is sometimes to dispose of deliberately, or be coerced to disregard, all that culturally decides their identities, and their individuality as people.

Notions that people who appear different should become like the dominant group are not new. From inception the history of the United States is one of assimilation with relatively recent examples such as the Irish, Germans, Italians and Jews in the nineteenth century and more recent immigrant groups from across the globe. But it is also the history of people choosing not to assimilate. Many groups, although often maintaining their cultural identities, manage to submerge themselves within American society. Nevertheless, groups such as Orthodox Jews remained highly visible and culturally separate through choice. For people of color the option of blending into society is for many virtually impossible because of skin color which has always branded them as different and for many inferior.

Multiculturalism in the 1980s and 90s was touted as a rejection of the assimilationist paradigm which would transcend tolerance. Members of the education research community and activists agitated for the reform of school curricula from a Eurocentric position to curricula inclusive of other cultures. This they believed would lead to greater academic success for multicultural students and in turn create better futures. For some the easy answer of adding "relevant curricula" to solve all issues was an exceptionally logical but naïve and lazy argument.

Critics talked of this as often token and trivial. To simply change a few aspects of the curriculum was nominal inclusion, and superficial; as something given without the marginalized having a voice in the proceedings means any recognition gained will often only last until someone more powerful comes along (Said, 1993). Adding "relevant" content material to the curriculum was a first step in changing education. But for real acceptance and alteration to occur attitudes and values would need transforming, along with the power structures surrounding schools and a recognition of the competition of different multicultural groups vying for an ever-decreasing piece of the pie of limited resources.

Progressive multiculturalism demanded new ways of looking at a society in every facet of its past and present. Therefore, from the late 1960s and the 1970s the multicultural movement in the United States was not only "to include more information about the culture and history of cultural groups in the social studies curriculum, but also to infuse the curriculum with new perspectives, frames of reference, and values" (Banks, 1991, p.133). This had some success, and histories of people of color were introduced, but placed into distinct times on the calendar, such as Black History month and Cinco de Mayo.

But the panacea of recognition and affirmation is limited. Representation in most American textbooks of people of color was still marginal well into the new millennium. Furthermore, White teachers, if they included knowledge about diverse groups, tended to do so in a haphazard fashion within a Eurocentric framework. Present-day research shows the mere inclusion of racially and ethnically diverse people in the curriculum has a limited effect as racial attitudes are habitually learned actively (Hughes, 2007; Sleeter, 2011).

The vantage point of the present also enables you to see one of the main challenges of the past and the teaching of multicultural material is the unpreparedness of many teachers to teach without reverting to mainstream accepted stereotypes and deficit narratives (Asher, 2007; Kymlicka, 2012). History, like memory, is an indispensable function that societies and individuals use to help create social and personal identities. You often hold views concerning the past that you take from a variety of sources including other disciplines and general culture. Consequently, what is learned in history classes might be just another "voice" in the "polyphony heard" and perhaps not the loudest or most convincing.

The pivotal function histories play within society and their social and psychological benefits are perhaps hard to deny. Evidence based research indicates the importance of diverse history curricula in societies; it also suggests strongly that children at school hold a complex array of ideas about history received from formal and informal sources.

This chapter was intended to give the reader an improved understanding of why the prior knowledge of history students of color may hold is significant, and why these students may often accept, reject, or remain apathetic to the history that they are taught. The research here demonstrates that the reasons are multiple and complex, but of crucial importance to history in education and democratic societies.

At the center of this book are assertions made by ethnically diverse students who think learning histories rich in aspects they can connect with culturally and personally are commonly important and necessary in gaining and holding their attention. Knowing this, the implications of how you teach history and what you teach as history become much clearer. Attention is a prerequisite for learning. Scientific experiments show uninteresting or irrelevant information is stored differently in the brain, and any student is presumably likely to recall elements of information they think important because of previous experience or attachments.

As long ago as the early 1970s Fisher's research discovered an absence of culturally relevant history created cultural amnesia and damaged the identity and self-esteem of individuals (Fisher, 1972). Furthermore, the ability to relate personally and identify with what is learned is an important prerequisite in the process of learning. This is a crucial finding and a basic argument underpinning this book. "Our emotions are integral to learning. When we ignore the emotional component of any subject we teach, we deprive students of meaningfulness" (Caine and Caine, 1994, p. 64) because

> we do not simply learn things. What we learn is influenced and organized by emotions and mind sets based on expectancy, personal biases and prejudices, degree of self-esteem, and the need for social interaction. Emotion and cognition cannot be separated. (Caine and Caine, 1994, P. 90)

CHAPTER THREE

Cognitive and Affective Factors and Possible Impact on the Learning of Multicultural Students

> History would give me a better understanding of things I am not too sure about. It would give me like solid ground to stand on.
>
> (Teresa, 15)

What is going on in the minds of students as they learn? In a classroom setting you often see a one- or two-dimensional picture of students at the start of the school year. As you get to know them, and they you, a more detailed picture begins to develop of who they are, or what they choose to let you see. The usefulness of traditional psychological theories is they enable you to gain a more detailed picture and a fuller understanding of the "inside feel" of students. This chapter summarizes theories about motivation, self-concept, attitudes and how they may influence the learning processes for students of color.

Extrinsic and Intrinsic Motivation

The word "motivation" is often used in conjunction with learning. But what is it? The first thing to be aware of about the concept is its complexity. When you begin to try to peel back the layers of the concept you find motivation has no ultimate definition. A key theory suggests (Atkinson, 1957) motivation is the result of an emotional conflict between striving for success and the fear of failure, and a drive toward a goal or the satisfying of a need. Most theorists agree there are two kinds of motivation: intrinsic and extrinsic. Both are recurrently pertinent to education.

You are often said to be extrinsically motivated when you engage in activity expecting a reward, or to avoid a punishment. In contrast intrinsic motivation comes from a desire to accomplish a task successfully, and irrespective of whether you may be punished or rewarded you think it is enjoyable. Intrinsic motivation is frequently fueled by attitudes toward what you are doing.

Learning is said to be more effective if students are repeatedly intrinsically motivated to be creative and solve problems. Evidence from research and personal experience suggests students tend to experience intrinsic motivation when they can frequently see what they are learning is relevant, interesting, or has some potential utility for life beyond school. Furthermore, they not only have to find what they are doing has value and matters, but they also need to feel competent and a measure of self-determination. Therefore, they need to be given choices.

However, increasingly school students are forced to participate in a variety of tests and targets, and this probably lessens intrinsic motivation for schoolwork. Teachers wanting to increase their students' intrinsic motivation in classroom tasks need to create academic environments promoting students' feelings of both "competence" and "control."

Fearing Failure

When students are successful or unsuccessful at a given task, they may believe their success or failure comes from either "internal" factors such as ability, effort and strategy or "external" factors like luck, difficulty and unfairness. When you blame failure on external reasons you may see the inability to complete a task as out of your hands as you are probably unable to change the situation. (If the teacher does not like you, then she is always going to give you low grades no matter what you do, so why try?)

Students who fear failure may attempt to escape it at all costs by avoiding situations where they know there is a high chance of failure. To illustrate this, recently, the day before a final college exam a student emailed her professor to say her pet had been diagnosed with a terminal illness, and so she could not take the exam as she had been too distressed. Telling her the test was mandatory and that she had been aware of it for some weeks, she arrived for the test and failed it. The professor was very bemused when she then asked if she could be given an "'A' due to extenuating circumstances."

In a classroom situation a fear of failure may mean some disruptive or uncooperative students are perhaps protecting themselves from failure. If a history curriculum excludes or presents certain cultural groups as invisible or recipients rather than actors this may be unwittingly casting them as failures, unimportant, and reinforcing certain views in society about multicultural groups among all students.

Motivational Processes

Theories about motivation suggest motivational processes determine the direction and the intensity of any behavior directed toward a goal or the drive to engage in a particular activity. There is no agreement on which or how many of the processes are necessary for motivation to function, but at least four processes are said to be at play when you are motivated toward something. You habitually need to feel a measure of control and competency or mastery at what you have been asked to do; novelty and curiosity need to be aroused; there has to be a directing component and a reward or fear of punishment; your intention is also an important factor determining motivation.

There are various kinds of learning at play in classrooms—"deep" and "surface" learning are probably highly significant. Students with a deep approach to what they are learning frequently want to reach a personal understanding of their schoolwork. A student with a surface approach often just wants to satisfy course or task requirements and their learning will probably be very shallow. The author once overheard a couple of students meticulously working out the minimum assignments and class attendance they needed to do to successfully complete their courses. It seemed clear from their discussion some classes would be approached in a very superficial manner.

In fairness to these students, this is something everyone is probably guilty of at some time. That is the experience of learning something for a test, and promptly forgetting most of what was learned once the test was over. Simply put, if your intention was superficial your learning will probably also be superficial. Furthermore, the reasons you may have for being motivated to engage in an activity may change over time (Weiner, 1972; Volz and et al., 2019).

You may, for example, escape into the garden because your partner is irritating you. Every time the irritation occurs you make your way into the garden and potter around. After a while you may find yourself going into the garden because you enjoy working there and not just as a place of refuge. Your motivation has changed. Of course, these are intricate and subtle arguments, but they do illustrate the importance of motivation, and why cognitive and affective concerns influence learning.

Students who are habitually engaged in their work display certain characteristics: they are frequently attracted to their work, they persist despite adverse circumstances, and they take visible delight in finishing set tasks. Teachers probably easily recognize when this is happening in their classrooms. If students of color are to be engaged when studying history or any other subject, they must feel some attraction, and a measure of ownership of the work they are given. If not, they may not persevere with the task or if they participate their learning may be shallow and half-hearted (Schlecty, 1994).

Most agree there is no full agreement in research about how motivation works. There are those arguing rewards are no better than punishments on behavior, especially for children (Kohn 1993). Others say dividing motivation into intrinsic and extrinsic fields has pitfalls, claiming if you look at the work of highly creative people you see a blend of both kinds of motivation, so both are of value to creativity and learning.

Still others argue that extrinsic rewards should be avoided when students are intrinsically motivated to do something. Nevertheless, few would disagree successful learning usually incorporates something attractive, stimulating and satisfying in some way to the learner. Most educators want to establish "intrinsic" and "deep" learning motivational attitudes in their students (Deci and Ryan, 2000).

What you can say about motivation with some authority is

- it is a multifaceted concept of great significance to people working in or wanting to understand how the learning process works
- there are no easy, foolproof ways of establishing motivation in a direction
- being aware of the principles and characteristics of motivation will aid both teachers and students in effective teaching and learning.

The ultimate motivational aim of most educators is to establish "intrinsic" and "deep" learning motivational attitudes in their students (Marton & Salijo, 1984; Ramsden, 1992; Biggs, 2003, Volz et al., 2019). In a data-driven education environment at times this may seem like wishful thinking and students having a desire to accomplish a task successfully irrespective of the rewards and punishments associated with it a distant reality. Helping students to develop enduring understandings about their learning rather than shallow surface learning for the end of semester examination is nevertheless a primary goal.

Educators know that intrinsic motivation is probably fueled by the attitudes that individuals have toward the subject matter in question, and may realize the necessity of guiding students toward a better personal understanding of how their attitudes toward a lesson/topic influence their learning experiences.

The Nature of the Self-Concept

The notion of self is broad and includes the "self-concept" and the "ideal self." Research on the development of the self-concept asserts it is not just made up of the slow accumulating of experiences, conditionings and definitions of others, but rather it is a configuration. Moreover, if one aspect of this configuration changes it may alter the nature of the whole (Rogers, 1989). Therefore, changing attitudes may also alter the concept of self.

People often develop complex personal constructs through experiences; this network of cognitive structures is what they usually use to make decisions about the most suitable behavior to meet past and present situations. All this suggests what students of color experience outside and inside their history classroom is likely to influence their concept of self and their behavior.

All facets of the self-concept are tangled up in the learning process. Self-efficacy, another part of the self-concept, may play a dominant role in educational attainment.

Self-Concept and Self-Esteem

The attitudes students of color have toward learning and how they perceive themselves and think others see them is a significant part of this book. And, interestingly, how students perceive themselves and their ability may have more of an impact on academic performance than actual ability. However, within education the precise relationship between attitudes and approaches to learning has not been fully identified. One seemingly valuable aspect in this respect is recognizing the notion of the self-concept is likely to be an important variable within which attitude function may be linked to learning.

Understanding the concept of self means understanding the subjective experiences of individuals—that is, knowing the individuals on their own terms. It is an intimate study of the individual. Traditional psychology argues, in order to study the self-concept, you must presume what it is like by observing what people do, such as behavior. And the self-concept appears to be influenced by your traits and values, together with the attitudes and perceptions you feel others have of you (Bills et al., 1951, pp. 257–261).

Researchers often divide the self-concept into three areas: self-image, ideal self, and self-esteem. The self-image is what you think you are; ideal self is what you would like to be; and self-esteem refers to the value you place upon yourself in terms of the discrepancy between your ideal and actual self-image. This is crucial when we look at the way students of color and other diverse students' self-esteem may be affected by how they think and feel during lessons.

High self-esteem alludes to a high estimation of one's own value, abilities and potential. Low self-esteem can involve harsh self-judgments for past experiences and low expectations for future achievements. Claims are made of students with high self-esteem consistently performing better than students of similar ability who have low self-esteem.

Psychological theories suggest students with high self-esteem set higher goals, show less need for adult approval, are often less deterred by failure and have a more realistic view of their own abilities. If history lessons are repeatedly exposing students of color to negative or invisible portrayals of minorities in history, high self-esteem is hardly likely to be fostered.

Present-day Western society habitually values the individual in terms of their ability to achieve competitively. Because society places great stress on the importance of academic and vocational achievements, failure and success in these areas is of paramount importance to individuals and how they view themselves. Researchers find, and many teachers would probably agree, nothing often contributes more to a student's sense of self-efficacy or self-esteem than succeeding at a task, nor shatters it so completely as failure, especially repeated failure (Rosenberg, 1965).

Age and Self-Concept

Why is age significant in relation to self-concept? First, it is important because age factors into the way self-concept develops. Adolescence is a crucial time as it marks the period when self becomes more aware of what "I" can become. An understanding of how age functions demonstrates that it is imperative to give ample opportunity to adolescents to find out who they are or may become. They frequently also need room to create positive self-concepts which are motivationally and ultimately academically significant. Success and seeing yourself as successful are crucial for motivation.

The attitudes of students of color toward learning and how they perceive themselves and think others see them is a significant part of this book. A person understands others and themselves through cultural stories or through meanings and practices that are often multiple and contradictory. Therefore, the narratives that students of color encounter at home and in schools and society are vitally important for their construction of self.

The reader is reminded that self-esteem refers to the value we place upon ourselves in terms of the discrepancy between our ideal and actual self-image. Considering this, the self-esteem of students of color is affected by how they think and feel during lessons. High self-esteem alludes to a high estimation of one's own value, abilities and potential. Low self-esteem involves harsh self-judgments for past experiences and low expectations for future achievements. Researchers have found that students with high self-esteem consistently perform better than students of similar ability who have low self-esteem.

Psychological theories suggest students with high self-esteem set higher goals, show less need for adult approval, are often less deterred by failure and have a more realistic view of their own abilities (McDonald and Jessell, 1992; Munson, 1992). If history lessons are repeatedly exposing students of color to negative or invisible portrayals of Black and brown people in history, high self-esteem is hardly likely to be fostered.

Conversely students are usually quick to spot fake praise and therefore affirming them, it seems, is best if the affirmation accurately evaluates their performance. The author uses the word "usually" because the proliferation of television programs such as Britain/America's got talent and idol shows thrive on auditions demonstrating just how far from reality many contestants are at estimating their "talent" and often being supported by family and friends seemingly oblivious to reality. Present-day Western society values the individual in terms of their ability to achieve competitively. Because society places great stress on the importance of academic and vocational achievements, failure and success in these areas is of paramount importance to individuals and how they view themselves.

Some self-concept theorists claim the self-concept is the most important phenomenological object within the experience of everyone because of its "primacy, centrality, continuity, and ubiquity in all aspects of behavior" (Weber, 1992, p. 52). So how does the self-concept work?

Self-Efficacy and Educational Attainment

When you examine work on how students learn you see cognitive processes play a significant role in receiving and holding on to any new behavior patterns. Cognitive processes ultimately preserve and strengthen your perception of how efficient you usually are at a task (Bandura, 1977). Teachers realize and recognize, at the start of any learning experience students' perceptions of self-efficacy vary considerably.

As students begin to work, they often derive cues from task engagement variables which signal just how well they are doing, and they use this information to assess their efficacy. If students of color or any students for that matter are repeatedly not attracted to their history work, they may be less likely to derive cues of engagement or signals of efficacy from what they are doing.

Importantly, research also shows a strong correlation between certain aspects of memory and self (Rogers et al., 1977). Frequently, when you are presented with information relating to self it is a highly effective strategy for remembering because information which is related to self appears to have a privileged place in memory, probably because of the egocentric character of knowledge (Greenwald and Pratkanis, 1988, p. 139). This is significant, because it assumes students given information relating to themselves may well experience improved motivation toward academic performance and enhance their self-esteem (McCarthy, 1994, pp. 289-305).

However, this begs the question of whether multicultural students are likely to be motivated *away* from performing academically if information relating to self is presented in such a way that it discourages or damages self-esteem. A further crucial notion is that you commonly only become aware of self-image when it is frustrated. When the self is violated it becomes a motivator. Seeing "self as motive" in this way makes sense.

Your motivation is aroused in the face of deprivation or when faced with contradictory roles. If you are presented with conflict, frustration, deprivation, or a shortfall in confidence, then self becomes a motivator.

Possible selves have a significant effect on academic achievement, which may play a salient role in delinquent behavior. Young adults who are frequently "able to construct and maintain a compelling set of possible selves will be better equipped to negotiate a relatively smooth transition to adulthood (Oysermann and Markus, 1990, p. 145)." On the other hand, "Those adolescents without a clear sense of who they are, and what is potentially important, valuable, distinctive, or special about themselves will have problems trying to elaborate a set of satisfying and believable possible selves" (Oysermann and Markus 1990, pp. 153–4).

This is very pertinent. If history lessons repeatedly fail to provide students of color with tools for constructing expected possible selves, then they may limit and impede some of these students from attaining their full potential, and these students may feel the need to look for possible selves that societies may find unnerving.

The Black Self-Concept

So far you have been looking at European psychological theories to explain the way Black and other students of color may perceive themselves, but some argue these theories do not fully address the Black self-concept, the argument being people of color may have attitudes peculiar to themselves which Eurocentric psychology does not or cannot recognize.

Of interest is the work of Markus and Kitayama (1991) and Nobles (1992), who find the self-concept varies among cultures. Markus and Kitayama debate whether Westerners typically view themselves as "independent" stable entities. African and Asian societies, they assert, see the self-concept as "interdependent" and connected with its social context. Western individuals picture the self as autonomous, consisting of unique traits. However, Markus and Kitayama make it clear the distinctions between independent and interdependent construal are general tendencies when the members of the culture are viewed.

The consequences of the African Diaspora are often cited as having affected the traditions of both Whites and Africans. However, these theories stress the diaspora did not result in a destruction of all things African. (You only need to explore the history and lifestyles of countries like Brazil to see just how much of Africa remains in the culture). The main point in understanding traditional African concepts of self is the belief "I am because we are; therefore, I am" (Mbiti, 1970). Furthermore, some researchers suggest because the Black self-concept is filtered through a European world-view, the validity of the Black self-concept is distorted. Therefore, if the Black self-concept is to be properly understood, it must incorporate African-based analysis and conceptualizations.

You could of course argue this position is also a stereotype. If this theory is valid then some Black students may reject the notion of individual competition, such as competition for exam results, because commonly they do not feel these things are of value. However, others will point to this being at odds with the reality of a significant number of young Black students heavily involved in competitive sports. Others may say this is largely due to the influence of many sports role models seeming to suggest to students of color that they can find success in this area.

Inclusion often creates involvement. Inclusion also raises the possibility of establishing or imagining "possible selves" for Black and other multicultural students. (The concept of possible selves will be fully discussed in chapter 4). Other less controversial research points toward the importance of social identity for the self-concept.

Social Identity

The idea of social identity is that you often need to identify with a cultural or micro-cultural group, and this identification may vary in strength from person to person. Social identity theory gives us a deeper understanding of the issues you have been examining. The theory concerns all aspects of group relationships, especially between groups having unequal power. Tajfel (1981, p. 255) defines self-identity as "that part of the individuals' self-concept which derive from their knowledge of their membership of a social reference group (or groups) together with the value and emotional significance attached to membership."

This theory assumes you are usually motivated to keep or realize positive self-identities and in a group situation you will commonly want to be part of a reference group enjoying high social status. Considering this, you make social comparisons between your group and other groups. These comparisons frequently determine the extent to which your own group furnishes you with a distinct positive social identity. If the comparisons you make between your group and another group lead to negative social identification, then you will probably feel dissatisfied, and may try to change the inter-group situation if it is perceived as unstable or unfair.

This has implications for multicultural groups who may find it impossible to change the inter-group situation because of ethnicity or gender. Studies on social categorization and memory conclude you tend to recall both similarities and differences about in-group members but remember only differences about out-groups. In a culturally diverse teaching environment an awareness of this phenomenon is probably useful if you are truly attempting to bring about inclusion in the classroom.

Several studies have explored the development of self-concept from infancy onward. For example, as you age you face critical challenges and must establish and re-evaluate your role in society (Erikson, 1968). Older people frequently must create a new self in whom competence and activity are habitually hallmarks. If they don't do this they may face feelings of disintegration coupled with a loss of motivation. In terms of the present work the largest group being explored are adolescents.

Adolescence is a crucial period because it marks the period when the self becomes more aware of what "I" is capable of becoming. It therefore seems imperative you give ample opportunity to all the students that you teach to find out who they are and may become. Students also need room to create positive self-concepts which may prove to be motivationally and ultimately academically significant. Success and seeing yourself as successful is the lifeblood of motivation. A final exploration of the self as a socially constructed entity completes this brief foray into an elaborate concept.

A Social Constructionist Perspective of Self

The idea of social construction theory is that everything you do is constructed through what a society views as normal values and customs. For example, the idea of being male and male traits in some societies may conjure up images of toughness, courage and "big boys don't cry" assertiveness. Women, on the other hand, are "supposed" to be delicate, kind and more thoughtful and empathetic. Basically, language ascribes social values in society. You understand your world through commonly understood, categories and concepts, and they are dependent on your specific culture and your specific histories (Burr, 2003). You are constructed socially.

Traditional psychological interpretations view the self as separate and private from the world around it (although some recognize African "selves" may involve greater interdependence). Conversely, social constructionists would argue the two are interwoven, and the way you relate to the world are functions of association, dialogue, and understandings about self, and are incorporated as part of a private world making up "the mind." The self is being continually shaped and reshaped through interactions with others and by involvement in social and cultural activities.

The person, consciousness, mind and self are all seen as social, so to argue certain aspects of self are determined from external influences and others by internal influences is pointless. Social constructionists say consciousness and self come about from socially and culturally organized meanings and practices. Furthermore, although you may have a strong sense of a self-contained world in your head, the reality of it is you take up bits and pieces of your public world and these become incorporated within the self and make up part of your private world.

Your understanding of others and yourself comes through cultural stories or through meanings and practices which, as stated previously, are often multiple and contradictory. Consequently, the narratives multicultural students encounter at home, in schools and in wider society are vitally important for their construction of self.

The social nature of the self is most evident when people from one culture are immersed in another strongly collectivist culture. Exploring cross-cultural differences in concepts of the self and in the psychological responses suggests the importance of the social situation in constructing human psychology. It used to be said cross-cultural research was problematic because of the difficulties in translating, but there is now ample evidence from a variety of researchers from around the world that the concepts of what it is to be a person varies across cultures such as Japan, Africa and the United Kingdom (Markus and Kityama 1991).

Recent work on intercultural competence points to several imperatives for becoming versed in cross-cultural interpersonal communication, and the issues arising for global understanding if ignored. Social constructionists theorize the cultural differences you find are crucial for understanding concepts of the inner life such as emotions, beliefs, and attitudes.

You make up your identity from the discourses culturally available to you. Your identity forms "not from inside the person, but from the social realm, a realm where people swim in a sea of language and other signs" (Burr,

2003, p. 109). You acquire "self" as you develop language representing the "structuring of experience" which has "internal logic, underlying categories, metaphors, and so on of the language we use" (Burr, 2003, p. 139). The self is structured in language. Memories, dreams, emotions are structured in language in a narrative form.

The way educators may unthinkingly use academic language in classrooms has come under scrutiny relatively recently and there has been a great push to recognize and teach students the meanings of discipline-specific language which is often lost in translation for students and particularly minority students for whom English is an additional language (Zwiers, 2008).

An example of the social constructionist theory of self is seen in the work of discourse analysis. Until relatively recently, most people probably readily assume language and discourse are used to describe "reality," words have fixed unambiguous meanings and you can infer inner states such as beliefs, attitudes, traits and emotions from the language you use. Discourse analysis argues reality and consciousness are constructed through language, and language is not a transparent medium for conveying thought but constructs the world and the self as it is being used. The theory of social constructionism takes much from literary theory and involves taking up a "deconstructive" perspective.

First and foremost, this theory is significant when you look at the way children mature. Children develop as social beings through being immersed in language into particular social and cultural processes. You coo words to babies and you point and show toddlers things and attach words to them. Second, children are also intimately involved in their own social construction and interwoven in the ongoing construction of their cultures.

Go to kindergarten and look and listen to children as they often play, mimicking the world around them. Narratives allow children to explore and negotiate a variety of beliefs and values, and to represent themselves in different ways. Children are from the start negotiating power relationships through dialogues in which they are involved, and which position them in certain ways. This positioning is an important aspect of the emerging social person.

This brief journey into the self-concept demonstrates its complexity, and just how vital it is if you are to grasp and gain a better understanding of how students may be feeling and thinking as they learn. A primary role for educators, policy makers and the like should habitually be striving and achieving optimum understanding of how all students learn best, then implementing research-based changes in education and facilitating more effective teaching and learning. That said, this chapter on "the inside feel" is incomplete without examining attitudes and the way they probably function in the context of learning.

The Role of Attitudes in Processing Learning

Recognizing the relevance of attitudes stems partly from traditional psychological theories, suggesting attitudes guide the way information is processed. Attitudes appear to help us in defining social groups, establishing identities, and guiding thinking and behavior. Most important for this work is the effect of attitude on memory.

Studies dealing with the process of "remembering" indicate it involves selection and the active reconstructing of material rather than "photographic" reproduction (Wertsch, 2002). Work by the Hovland group at Yale focused on how you process information; this processing can be either central or peripheral. If the message you receive is very relevant, you are more likely to process it centrally and to be convinced by crucial factors like quality of argument. If the message habitually has low relevance for you or if you are distracted while processing the information, the information will regularly be processed peripherally.

You may have seen the video of people being asked to count how many times a ball is passed to them in a circle. At the end of the game the participants can recall how many times the ball was caught, but not the gorilla that walks through the group in the middle of the game. In other words, frequently messages that are not deemed as relevant will often have less significance for learners who will probably not recall such information easily.

Essentially, this research also suggests the way you organize things cognitively and your reflective awareness may be influenced by the attitudes you hold. You are often more likely, for example, to be persuaded by information not going against previously held attitudes. Therefore, you may watch a television channel that supports your political beliefs and values and reject channels that you do not agree with. It seems reasonable to argue these findings about attitude processing are probably pertinent for people involved in education, particularly those teaching students of color. The perceived relevance of history lessons for students may be a key factor in their retention of knowledge and for gaining and keeping their engagement (Eiser, 1986).

In a knowledge heavy subject like history, this is crucial. Also perhaps even more critical is that teachers may unwittingly be reinforcing negative attitudes students already hold about multicultural groups.

Attitudes and Behavior

Unfortunately—and from an educator's point of view, infuriatingly—consciously held attitudes do not always correspond with behavior. It would be convenient if attitudes mirrored behavior but this is clearly not the case. Consciously held attitudes appear to set "ideal" standards beyond the reach of individuals. The usefulness of attitude tests may be called into question, as in theory they may demonstrate very little about the way in which you behave in circumstances when facing the opportunity to live up to a consciously held attitude.

For example, you may have a guilt attitude toward ice cream being detrimental to your health, but when facing the temptation of a plate of vanilla or chocolate chip goodness, you may well indulge and then feel guilty about your "failure." But the guilt concerning eating the ice cream fails to deter you from eating it on another occasion. Importantly, attitudes appear to be more consistent with behavior when they are frequently strongly held, specific to identifiable circumstances, and based on direct experience.

Approaches for Encouraging Attitude Change

The implications of recognizing and using the existing knowledge on attitudes to improve learning are commonly important for education. Nevertheless, within educational circles many often appear reluctant to apply attitude research findings as tools, perhaps thinking the manipulative possibilities are probably too dangerous. However, for teachers and researchers, the need to encourage or recognize attitude change in those you teach and with whom you work is ever present. The fact of the matter is that existing attitudes must be undone if different attitudes are to be constructed.

When you discuss you use cognitive reasoning and a shift in the balance of forces for and against may change an attitude, highlighting the necessity in allowing time for discussing sensitive topics as salient if you want to encourage attitude change in history classrooms and lecture halls (Lewin, 1948; Beckett, 2009).

Lastly we turn to brain-based research which has become more influential in terms of the potentialities it may have with regard to education.

Brain-Based Research

The impact of the environment on the brain has taken on real significance for education over the last three decades. Key findings concern the impact of how nurturing environments on the brain can make a significant difference in how it develops, suggesting that a classroom low on "threats" enhances the learning capacity of students, and classrooms that have stimulating environments improve learning. If educators fail to cultivate classroom environments that stimulate, then one result for students will often be boredom. This is apparently not just a teenaged disposition but seems to have physical repercussions. When "teenaged" rats were exposed to boring environments their brain cortex became thinner, whereas stimulating environments thickened their cortex (Diamond and Hopson, 1998).

Of course, there are problems with accepting these theories as with any assumption. After all, teenaged students are not rats. It may seem a long way to jump from rats to humans, but can we really afford to ignore this research? Other findings in neuroscience studies suggest one of the necessary basic conditions for effective learning is mental challenge. Students who begin a topic with a negative attitude toward it, through prejudice of some kind are highly unlikely to feel mentally challenged in a positive manner. Therefore, the result for students is that little effective learning will probably take place.

Students are recurrently mentally challenged by the introduction of new knowledge, limiting the time they must complete a task and varying access and expectations. These all provide challenges which many students find stimulating. However, for positive student participation to occur interest must be aroused.

Encoding is the process a person uses for putting new (incoming) information into the brain that processes and prepares the information for storage—that is, long-term memory. For encoding to work at an optimum level, the new information must be meaningful. Usually only then will a person be being able to integrate it with previous information and store it in long-term memory. This implies that students frequently need to have some personal interest attached to what they are learning. Thus, they can make new information meaningful and integrate it into their long-term memory.

Interestingly for history educators, it seems the best way to grow the brain is to give it problems to solve. Surprisingly, the brain does not care if it cannot find answers to the challenges it is trying to overcome. It is the process and not the solutions that spur neuron growth. The brain needs feedback to reduce uncertainty and increase its coping abilities. Sadly, research informs us that students of color are frequently less likely than their White counterparts to receive feedback of a positive and academic nature. Neuroscience points out that pituitary-adrenal stress responses are lowered if the brain gets feedback.

Furthermore, even if the individual has no control over a situation, feedback is still valuable. The brain, much like a person on a familiar route, decides what is necessary based on what it has done previously. Without feedback the brain could not function, therefore, the necessity for feedback to be specific for the brain to function well. If you think of the way smart phones capture the attention, then you recognize it is feedback that holds the user captive. When educators grade work they should be giving specific feedback. When students work in groups they are often providing and provided a wealth of feedback for the brain, enabling them to learn more effectively and efficiently (Jensen, 1998).

It is students' experiences that generate emotions: anger, disgust, fear, surprise, sadness and joy all come from experiences. From these students habitually generate thoughts, opinions and make decisions. These then frequently generate a student's responses—whether they are confused, or cynical, or optimistic, or confident, or frustrated all these will probably strongly move a student to resist or engage in what they are learning. So, to ignore the emotional is often to cut off the foundations of how a student experiences what it means to be human in the classroom and life.

To conclude, all students probably have explicit or inexplicit notions about what history does or should do. This repeatedly impacts on their understanding of what history is about and what they expect to be learning. A partial understanding of these ideas may lie in the way they develop a sense of self, their mind-sets, and their expectancies. One of the traits of adolescents is they are frequently highly aware of self. Various theories agree adolescence is a crucial period when young people develop a sense of who they are, their identity in the social world, and this forms a framework for adulthood (Archer, 1994).

The collected histories of societies enable students to establish themselves in relation to other societies and to initiate a sense of security and orientation. Some theorists argue that embedded within each person is an intrinsic philosophy or world-view, a mind-set, which essentially molds how they see the world (Sire, 1997, p. 16). If this is accepted as a reasonable assertion then the newly evolving worldviews of young people are often malleable and can be impacted on during the learning process. Some students may think that the narratives they are being asked to accept are not what they classify in their intrinsic philosophies as their own. Their experiences may even suggest that some narratives are irrelevant.

The increasing diversity in our schools has and is producing a plurality of value systems and affective concerns requiring consideration and respect from society; especially those involved in education. Admittedly some students are more likely than others to encounter dissatisfying learning experiences in history classrooms, because of previously held attitudes, whether their own or others. It may follow such students are more likely to be less motivated to engage positively with what they are being taught in their history lessons, as "feelings and fantasies are just as powerful sources of human motivation and action as interests or rational calculations" (Greven, 1984, p. 72).

CHAPTER FOUR

Students of Color Talk About the Role and Purpose of History in Their Lives

History is for knowing your roots and where you come from.

(Martin, 15)

Fact Finding Interviews

In empty classrooms with orange plastic chairs, behind the stage in a screened off section of a school assembly hall, in a home economics room in the small sparsely furnished apartment where the skills of cooking and ironing are taught along with the making of Victoria Sandwich cakes and Bakewell Tarts students talk freely about what they thought of the history they were studying and what they thought history was for. As they talked, what they acknowledged as being significant in their experience of school history and history from external sources emerges.

Talking About School History

All the students, seven girls and six boys, were between the ages of 15 and 17. They were all Black, of African and Caribbean, Bi-racial Mixed White and Caribbean heritage. The boys sported high-top hairstyles and the girls wore braided, relaxed and natural hair. One had experienced middle school in the United States, but the others had all been educated in the United Kingdom. Interviewer questioning covered a range of topics. Students talked about their interests and frustrations, their likes and dislikes, about the past and school history lessons in general.

The interviews provided insights into a range of students' ideas, experiences and expectations of school history. In them there was a distinct dichotomy in the way these students thought history operated, which contrasted with their experiences. It was soon clear that for the majority learning history was clearly fulfilling both personal and social functions. Not unsurprisingly students talked about wide-ranging issues. It was expected that there would be a sharp divide on specific applications of history, but the extent to which they agreed was surprising. Students spoke about history helping them in a variety of ways, and themes emerging included ideas about

1. Identity, perspective and interpretation
2. Personal and social knowledge
3. Perspective and historical explanation
4. Personal and social interest

History Is for Helping Us Understand the Contemporary and a Guide for Future Action

Dealing with students' conceptions of the role and purpose of history in society and in history in education it is very apparent that they all believed the past directly affected the present and the possible future. Gisella, (16) bubbly and thoughtful, stated a key function of Black history is its ability to establish a sense of identity for Black people—who they are, and where they are going:

> Yes I believe it (Black History) is necessary because Black people on the whole will be able to know more about their roots, and where they are coming from, and to gain inspiration for tomorrow. It could also motivate their attitude towards others by knowing about Black history.

This emphasis of seeing the role of history as being one which constructs from the inside outward demonstrates the social constructionists' view of the self.

Memory

History is a memory heavy subject. One of the most common anecdotal complaints about history is "having to remember all those dates." Importantly, research shows a strong correlation between certain aspects of memory and self (Rogers et al., 1977). Often when we are presented with information relating to self it is a highly effective strategy for remembering because information which is related to self appears to have a privileged place in memory, probably because of the egocentric character of knowledge (Greenwald and Pratkanis, 1988, p. 139).

If habitually we are not exposing our students to experiences and stories not only about themselves but about other societies, then we are doing them a disservice. For example, in 2016 Phi Delta Pi Record published an article about the scant weight given by pre-service teacher preparation courses and in-service teacher professional development to the "issue of culturally responsive teaching." It claimed that there was an emphasis on "helperism," a deficit narrative with a savior-like mentality of wanting to rescue students from their shattered communities. (Zeichner, 2016).

In the closing years of this decade it is clearly seen that there have been improvements in teacher preparation programs with regard to issues of inclusion, diversity and equities. But are they changing the way students view different cultures? What impact if any this is having on the way these pre-service students teach in the classroom, and about other regions of the world is a question yet to be adequately answered.

Clearly in these interviews, students believed knowing history was a means of creating a sense of solidarity and connections between the present and the past. A key function of learning history, they thought, was to inspire piety for their ancestors' experiences and could be a motivating force for the Black community to achieve greater things.[1] Eartha (17) said learning history was teaching her to understand the present. She talked about the Los Angeles riots (1992) following the acquittal of officers seen beating Rodney King, and the past and perhaps the future situation of Black people:

> Because I did Black history, it is easier to understand the situation now . . . what Black people had to go through, it makes you aware that being Black is not easy. . . . Our tribute to Black people of the past should be to carry on the civil rights and achieve goals greater than any other generation.

Other students talked of Malcom X, and images popular at the time, holding a rifle with the words "by any means necessary." Students' discussions of Black historical icons were spoken about reverentially. Malchus (17) commented:

> I think Malcolm X taught Black people how to have pride in themselves, as well as how to get on with other Black people, and that we have to get on with other Black people before we can get on with White people.

They shared their stories of Black historical figures as useful for pointing to contemporary problems and holding out possible solutions. Sometimes they recognized limitations, implying sections of society had more of a need to know Black history than others, Spencer (16) said, "certain people need to know about Black history, but to me it encourages too many arguments—for example, a Malcolm X versus Martin Luther King class discussion." Digging further he spoke of conflicts in the classroom, as sides were taken in debates and these had been for him disruptive, hinting the classroom atmosphere may have become charged and uncomfortable.

The theme *understanding the future and a guide for future action* is revealing of a focus that these students had, concerning issues of history helping Black people to create a sense of unity and solidarity. For them learning about people they considered their ancestors and how they coped under difficult circumstances was inspiring and offered them solutions for present-day challenges. The capacity of history to help them understand causes of problems in the present through looking at their origins and being able to locate and find a position in society shines through in their words. Tied to these notions and at times difficult to separate were ideas concerning identity, an issue which the students spent much time talking about.

Visible differences make blending into a country that sees itself as a White Anglo-Saxon society, mythical for people of color. If the new migrants abandon their cultural identifications and heritage, they will become free to participate in the national culture, which at worst is disingenuous and at best an oversimplification (Gilroy, 2002).

History Is for Telling Us Who We Are or Can Be

On both personal and social levels these students talked of history enabling Black people to create and affirm their identities. Entwined in their beliefs about history helping them to see who they are was the idea that history can change the way they view others and others view them. They indicated history should enable Black people to see themselves as part of a larger entity having a respected and recognized place in the world. Another clue to their thinking was the notion of it being unfair to be left ignorant about Black culture and heritage.

These students thought knowing their own history was a right. Students talked about instances of hurt and anger they experienced during history lessons as they learned about historical Black figures. Shaniqua, (16) speaking of a previous school, used the idea about ownership of history and the temporal extension of identity:

> I think every Black child should know their history. At my old school they made me feel bad about being Black when we did the slave trade. They talked about all the diseases that the slaves had. You should be proud about your history. They made me feel ashamed.

One of the strongest clues regarding the thinking these students had concerning history is that stories of suffering during slavery and other times were not affirming to Black people and were in fact belittling them. Furthermore, there was little doubt that they seemed to believe quite strongly history lessons should offer a "feel-good" factor. You see this emphasis when Shaniqua recounted a story of her experiences in one of the five secondary schools she had attended, more than one school per year:

> Shaniqua: When I first came here [to this school] all I knew about was slavery. Now I know about Malcolm X and people like Martin Luther King. . . . Before I came to this school I'd never heard of Martin Luther King.
>
> Interviewer: How did you find out about Malcolm X and Martin Luther King Jr.?
>
> Shaniqua: Through the media and through people I know who are in certain organizations.
>
> Interviewer: What do you mean by certain organizations?
>
> Shaniqua: I mean like, you know like there is a church and the things they talk about are the things Martin Luther King used to teach Black people. It's based in America where he was born and you know they have magazines talking about Martin Luther King and Malcolm X.

While studies appear to suggest perceptions of self-efficacy are probably a valuable predictor of student motivation and learning, another salient predictor of student motivation is the role "possible selves" play in perceived competence and self-regulation.

Possible Selves
Possible selves are your ideas about what you "might become," or what you are "afraid of becoming" or what you "would like to become." They contrib-

ute to motivation by providing you with specific goals for which you can strive, and they motivate through providing emotional energy to pursue your goals. If students of color are frequently presented with historical ancestor figures that are usually recipients of favors from others or classified as victims, or largely invisible, then their role models of historical possible selves are perhaps arguably being unnecessarily limited.

On top of this as mentioned in chapter 3, you only become aware of self-image when it is frustrated. When the self is violated in some way it becomes a motivator. If you experience conflict, frustration, deprivation, or a short-fall in confidence, then self becomes a motivator (Garcia and Pintrich, 1995). Possible selves have a significant effect on academic achievement, which as was mentioned before may play a crucial role in reckless behavior.

Clearly, if history lessons fail to provide multicultural students with tools for constructing expected possible selves, then this limits and places barriers around some of these students, preventing them from attaining their full potential. And to preserve their self-image, they may feel the need to often look for possible selves in other places that are showing them potentialities that some democratic societies may find unnerving and destructive to societal cohesion.

Shaniqua's experiences of history concerning Black people was that their history started in the fifteenth century with the slave trade and the Black person as victim; other aspects of Black histories in her experience were ignored. Shaniqua previously attended five secondary schools in London; however, school was not the only avenue that she had for learning history, as her comments on contacts with the American church indicated. Why five schools? Perhaps her parents were one of the many Black parents shopping around for an education that did not make their children educational casualties.

The options taken up by parents of color to "save" their children's education are often limited. They can try multiple schools, withdraw from the state sector, send their children back to ancestral homelands to be educated, attempt to fight the system from within, homeschool, or set up their own schools (Simon, 2005).

Many of the ideas that the students used mirrored those often found in society. Students talked about their need for personal utility in what they were taught and wanted to identify with strong positive role models. And they were quick to spot fake/surface inclusion, Ebbe (16) said:

> I think that it is essential for Black children to know their history. Not just pictures on the wall. Because it is not taught as much as White history in most

schools and Black children are not told the roles that Black people played in history, so they do not think they have achieved anything.

Hidden Histories

The idea of Black history being hidden was another strong idea present in students' conversations. The students talked with passion about Black children being ignorant of the achievements of Black people throughout time. They declared Black people in history were often portrayed as passive recipients of the actions of others and not actors. Ten of the students brought up the idea that a lack of active Black role models reinforces society's view of Black people as being underachievers and history lessons could help remedy this. They also shared instances of Black progress and a positive change in the way people of color were treated in society, but students still appeared to believe that there was room for improvement.

And for all of them the country of their birth was home. But their Black heritage was also an indelible part of their identity and they thought they had a right to study it. Twelve of the students talked about society's views of Black people, sometimes forcing them to acknowledge images of Black people that they were not comfortable with. Eleven students said positions assigned to Black people in history narratives were overwhelmingly negative and this reinforced the disapproving images of Black people students were finding in some sections of society.

As they talked individually a picture of their tiredness formed of being shown Black people as victims in history. You don't have to be a genius to realize they wanted to be taught some positive facts about Black people. They wanted to hear acts of heroism, not victimization. History, they thought, should tell stories about Black people who mastered technology and invented things. For years technology was king in society and students saw this. Using and mastering technology made people superior. Adara (15) speaks about what she perceives was often taught in history and what she thought should be taught:

> Blacks have been part of history since the world began, and when they teach about Blacks they teach about slavery and how terrible it was, but they don't teach about the great Black people . . . there are many who have invented all sorts of things.

Keith C. Barton (1996) notes students often equate technological changes with people becoming or being more intelligent, and similarly work by Lee and Ashby (2001) indicates this commonly held attitude of "technological progress" and the idea of "increasing knowledge and understanding" in the present day. These students believed that technological progress was a key feature of history, and maybe even a measure of worth, and the absence of Black technological achievement was a serious matter for them.

In apparent contrast, some students objected to the term "Black history." When asked if students should learn Black history Malik (16) became agitated, "No, history is history, Black people are a part of history, no, they should be taught as children that happen to be Black, not Black children." He continued, "It's vital for Black people to know where they are coming from. . . . We should teach history. Black people are a part of history. I think GCSE (General Certification of Secondary Education) should be world history, key dates and events in history." Malik refused the condescension that placed Black people in history into segregated pockets of the past.

Students' words also implied they acknowledged historical events had multiple meanings and often this depended on who was looking at them. One topic took a pole position in their conversations. Slavery. It was a problematic issue for several students. They knew all too well its horrors, and some students recognized it impacted in different ways on different cultural groups. A few students talked about a measure of reciprocity between Blacks and Whites coming out of slavery.

Malchus (17) said "slavery is something that happened which is important to everybody in the world." When asked "why"? Malchus replied, "Not only were Black people enslaved, but then White people had to accept them, the Black people, as their equals." As they spoke strong indications of students recognizing that prejudice and racism were not confined to Black versus White issues arose. Multicultural groups, they understood, were prone to discrimination or prejudice, be it for race, nationality or gender. These students did not see bigotry as the preserve of any group.

The conversations highlighted that issues of identity featured strongly in their minds when they were learning history. They believed history identified and affirmed them in their own eyes and in the eyes of others. Studying Black history for them was the "right" of all Black people and useful for White people. Half of them declared terms such as "Black history" marginalized the study of history in education. Twelve students talked about negative images of Black people in history creating stereotypes and reinforcing negative perceptions of Black people in society. The teaching of slavery was problematic.

Their views implied if history was well taught it would automatically include and affirm Black people. Moreover, they wanted history about Black people to become mainstream and not relegated as a side issue. Admittedly the students' preoccupation with issues of identity and negative historical images of Black people may have arisen from personal experiences. Was their emphasis on issues of identity prominent in their thinking because most were from a relatively recent migrant background or because of their visible differences to White British society?

History Is for Personal and Social Interest

High on the list of engaging topics for these students was fascism in Italy and Germany. However, Barnaby (17) disliked fascism in Italy because of the treatment of Ethiopia by Mussolini during the war between the two countries. This was surprising as in conversations with his teacher he admitted Mussolini's treatment of Ethiopia took up very little time during history lessons and was relegated to homework. In the interviews students latched on to the smallest details they thought were culturally relevant.

The emergence of a Communist State in China was remote and difficult for them to understand. It appeared the further away the country was from their everyday experience the greater the difficulty most students had with identifying and finding personal relevant points of contact with the topic.

Most students touched on race relations in the United States, some students experienced difficulties coping with this segment, but others enjoyed it. Eartha (17) listed several topics she found interesting and which increased her understanding of the world. Talking of "Black history," she declares it was history explaining Americans, not automatically equating Black American history with herself, which is what framers of the history curriculum seemed to suggest would happen for Black students.

The comments about lessons including Black historical figures were not all positive. Malchus (17) in answering the question of what he had liked and disliked most in his history lessons, retorted, "I liked Germany and China. I disliked race relations . . . because it made me angry, but if we did more I might be able to understand." Later on in the interview Malchus confessed to having stopped working in history lessons during that section of the course.

Malchus seemed unable to understand why he was angry or how to channel his anger. The root cause was vague and intangible, but he thought learning more about it might help him "understand." Perhaps not knowing how to cope with his anger, he responded in a manner that was potentially academically damaging.

History Is for Personal and Social Knowledge

Practical considerations of history populated the interview transcripts. History as a tool completing gaps of knowledge on the part of different cultural groups about their respective heritages was one prominent idea noticed, as was the belief that knowing history was important in terms of roots and locating themselves in society. Knowing Black history was an exception rather than the rule. These students talked at length of the ignorance of White people regarding people of color.

Students believed because White people were generally ignorant of Black history, they needed to be taught it. Ignorance, they suggested, caused many problems. They commented often that knowing the history of others created better understanding and broke down barriers within society. Desean (16) spoke on why he thought teaching Black history in schools was important:

> So we can find out more about ourselves. And in other schools [with a White student population] yes, because it will help young children and help White children to socialize with Blacks. We might be able to live with each other better, to solve problems.

Students declared there was social value and prestige in "knowing." Knowing had social kudos; it helped individuals fit in. A prevalent idea surfacing was that learning history might improve society and create greater understanding between cultural groups. On a practical level, students' ideas signified a function of history was establishing rules of conduct for individuals within society. They judged having some general knowledge about the way that society functioned in the past was a mark of achievement in society. Understanding the past reduced barriers and eased tensions. Barnaby (17) is meticulous in his dissection of why knowledge was power:

> [History was important] Yes, for everyone because, one, they can be more broad minded; never say no to knowledge. Two, the history that you study means that you won't stereotype the people that you deal with. Three, if you know about a person's history it will stand you in a good stead when dealing with that person. It's another notch in your belt.

Personal and social knowledge encircled ideas these students held about the importance of knowing. In practical terms the overwhelming consensus was that all children should learn about the histories of themselves and others, as this would help create social cohesiveness and understanding between ethnic groups. Did any of these ideas come directly or indirectly from parental emphasis on the value of education? Was the emphasis of society on the value of general knowledge a factor influencing the ideas of these students? Another possibility was that messages from society about the need for greater social cohesiveness were indeed filtering down to them (Levstik, 2000; Epstein, 1997).

Issues of Perspective and Historical Explanation

Linked to issues of identity were issues of perspective, which some students thought influenced the purpose and value of history. Perspective and historical explanation often appeared conflated in the minds of the students. They were repeatedly of the opinion that history was or could be taught with a specific purpose in mind. Seven of them thought history lessons should be taught to inspire and motivate.

Furthermore, six were of the opinion perspectives of White teachers were different and less sympathetic to issues in Black history than their Black counterparts. Most students assumed history could be taught from a neutral perspective and this would reveal the "truth" of the past. One key idea was learning history from a Black perspective.

All the students held ideas about historical explanation. Giselle, who had gone to school in America, said that in America "I did American history, but they don't teach about race relations unless you go to a predominantly Black school." Teaching from a "Black perspective" had its advantages in her mind. "If you are taught from a Black perspective you will know it is for you; a Black teacher won't fill your mind with negatives. Some White teachers tend to take things out, bits of Black people's history, and throw it here and there to make it look better."

A minority of students (three students from a total of thirteen interviewed) wanted history taught only from a Black perspective. Giselle did not elaborate on what she thought was a Black perspective. However, she seemed to take it for granted Black teachers would not teach Black history negatively. She thought Black teachers would be unafraid when they tackled emotive subjects in Black history.

However, Giselle's responses suggested she assumed some White teachers might be dismissive, or elaborate on, certain sections of history to the detriment of the subject. By using the words "to make it look better" she argued against condescension on the part of White teachers. She believed Black teachers were less likely to teach about Black people as victims and passive recipients in society.

Other students used ideas that agree with Giselle's. Dermot (16) speculated it might be refreshing to hear Black history from a Black perspective. "Yes, there are Black people who have probably only heard it from a White perspective in the past." Others said that they would find it difficult to accept Black history from a White teacher. Desean (16) was firm and strident when he exclaimed, "It should be biased; they should have a Black teacher teaching Black history. I would probably reject it from a White teacher—half the time I'd be thinking, no, I don't want to hear it from you."

For Desean only Black teachers had the right to teach Black history. When asked, "How do you feel about a Black teacher teaching European History?" Desean replied "No, that is all right, but the closest other schools get to Black history is Egypt, then stop right there. Black teachers get more involved. It would be difficult for a White person to dig for information." This will mirror findings by Epstein (1997) years later regarding African American students in the United States.

Desean implied Black teachers shared a common history, creating a bond. He thought White teachers would find it more of a challenge to research Black history than Black teachers. Most of the students suggested it was better to see different views. Eartha (17) spoke:

> History should be both ways, because taught from one perspective it can be corruptive. Even if the same thing carries on now we should see it in a better way. We should not be racist. We should be neutral.

Balance was important for these students. Most of them, like Eartha for example, thought history could be taught from a "neutral" point of view. Her ideas indicated she thought a person should be left to analyze history from as many angles as possible. In contrast to Eartha, Dempsey (15) referred to perspectives in a slightly different way, commenting, "I think they should be taught history from all perspectives, because people look at Black history in different ways and it is good for the person learning history to identify different views and feelings towards it."

The interviewer asked Dempsey where she had learned about Black history outside of school and she replied, "Well, mainly from a Black organization called Link, and from rap music and from my Mum." Dempsey's ideas differed from Eartha's as she did not talk about points of view but about interpretations. Her ideas were not unique; eight of the students implied histories could be interpreted from different angles and that people gained much more from history if they viewed it through multiple lenses.

These students' responses indicated they thought there should be no authorized versions of history and multiple views made for greater understanding. Furthermore, they viewed looking at history from different perspectives positively. Was this partly because of the influence of external information sources many had mentioned? Students also brought with them the idea that people saw things differently because of different social contexts.

Research by Barca (1996) on the ideas students hold about historical explanation are illuminating to some of the ideas expressed by the students. She found students demonstrated different levels of understanding about historical explanation, and detected some students thought the idea of different "perspectives" is "legitimate" and others voiced "concern for a tentatively perspectiveful neutrality" (p.108). Some students, along with seeing "tentative perspectiveful neutrality" in historical explanation, also recognize the possibility of the impact of "social context" on "point of view."

In these exploratory interviews multicultural students did have an awareness of the "legitimacy of perspectives" and appeared to appreciate the idea that different viewpoints might be dependent on social context. The students thought the way people perceived history depended on a variety of external and internal factors. And interestingly, most students believed that historical explanations could be made from a neutral perspective.

In summary, on issues of perspective and historical explanation most students were under the impression that history could be taught from a "neutral" stance and that balance was important. The ideas of the students called for inclusion, not exclusion. Spencer (16) perhaps sums this up when he proposed, "They [all students] should get a mixture of every type of history, that's the reason for race problems, not enough understanding of everyone's cultures."

Listening to what these students have to say gives tantalizing nuggets of ideas they hold about history and what it does and should do. Clearly visible are frequent indications of images of themselves students take from their history lessons and the personal feelings they experienced when taught history.

Of course, the number of students interviewed was small, but they do further understanding of probable reasons behind why many have viewed teaching culturally relevant history of critical importance to the academic and personal wellbeing of their children.

These interviews took place in the early 1990s. These children are Generation X, the forgotten generation, and some are now the parents and possibly grandparents of students we have in our history classrooms today.

Note

1. A notion somewhat similar to that of Walsh, (1992, pp. 35–44).

CHAPTER FIVE

Decoding Students' Ideas

If your ancestors were involved. I feel especially interested.

(Tolu, 13)

This chapter is based on the complex ideas of 124 students aged 13–16 which are codified, and their essence extracted. First an overview profile is presented of six students who are frequently representative of those who think their history lessons are ideal, satisfactory, or inadequate. This composite picture is demonstrative of students you may find in multicultural classrooms. Decoding their ideas and sifting through patterns of thinking and using the actual words of individuals gives a clearer picture of the differences you may find between cultural groups in their ways of thinking about their history lessons.

Student Profiles

The six students are Amanda, Martin, Susan, Tolu, John and Pauline,[1] (one Asian, two White and three Black). John, 15, reports "history is his favorite subject." Susan, 15, and Tolu, 13, write history is about the same as other subjects. Amanda, 14, and Martin, 15, write "history is their least favorite subject." and Pauline, 15, says "history was worse than most subjects." These are students you meet daily.

History Is Ideal
John (male, 15, White)

"I enjoyed it all. I love history because it's interesting and you get to learn about different things that happened all around the world." This is the student seeming to soak up everything in your history lessons. John has been influenced to choose history because his career goal is to be a historian. John says in class he concentrates "all the time." He knows a lot about history, and he often recalls things from the History Channel.

He likes talking to the whole class. John likes giving his opinions—he feels involved during "an oral lesson. We were put into small groups to study different areas of Russia during 1914 and 1917. Once the work was done, we had to read them out to the class. I felt really involved." You are very happy about his enthusiasm. He is always asking if you have seen some obscure film about the battle of something, and this is distracting for other students.

The lessons always "feel too easy" and he always feels "curious about the past." For John "all other subjects are less important than history."

History Is Satisfactory
Susan (female, 15, White)

"It is important we know about the past so not to make mistakes, have a knowledge of our past, so as not to fall into the same traps," writes Susan. You remember teaching Susan's sister a couple of years ago. She was a hard worker and you expect the same diligence from Susan. In class Susan works quietly and always hands in her homework on time. You know she is hoping to become a computer analyst. Susan reveals she chose history because, "it was my preferred subject to geography. Also my sister did well in history."

She does not want to continue studying history after school. In the survey Susan claims she concentrates nearly all the time in her history lessons and tends to agree history is an important subject to study. During her history lessons other students annoy her but she likes her teacher. The topics that engage her most are "lessons about the Jews in Germany because I felt I needed to know this. It quite shocked me about how badly they were treated. Also about women in Germany made me feel annoyed about how they were treated." You remember Susan asking a lot of questions during lessons on the Holocaust and sometimes perhaps she is silently drinking everything in.

Susan cannot think of anything making her feel alienated during history lessons. Compared with other subjects, history was "about the same."

Tolu, (male, 13, Black)

"History lessons are especially interesting because you learn about your ancestors and the past. If your ancestors were involved. I feel especially interested." This is the student you have who finds learning interesting. In class he occasionally whispers something to the person sitting next to him, but quickly goes back to his work. He says he concentrates much of the time in class. Talking with him he tells you he has several careers in mind, including "doctor, lawyer, engineer, or solicitor."

He does not want to study history when he leaves school. He strongly agrees history is an important subject to study. When you are teaching you may notice he is listening intently, he asks questions and nods in agreement or shakes his head in disbelief from time to time. During history lessons he says he feels "absorbed, interested, and aware of the past." He feels curious about the past and enjoys his history lessons.

You know that Tolu was born in Nigeria, he talks about his country proudly. He feels most involved when studying, "Black history and slavery, another subject was the emancipation of slaves and the American Civil War." Tolu writes he never feels alienated during history lessons, "I have never felt like this, it is just that some subjects are more interesting than others." Tolu concludes history was "about the same as other subjects."

History Is Inadequate
Amanda (female, 14, Asian)

"I think the work is mostly too hard and I hardly ever understand it. If I ever do it, it is still confusing, but I am really worried about history tests." Amanda is a typical fourteen-year-old and thinks she is working hard during her history lessons, but she is not working as hard as she could. You realize Amanda needs extra help if she is to pass her exams. As her teacher you wonder why Amanda chose to take history at examination level. You spend a lot of time explaining historical concepts and events to her. Amanda does not seem to understand.

She is bored by Hitler and the Second World War but likes when her teacher "jokes around." She writes a "friend" has influenced her to study history as an examinable subject. You notice she puts her head down on her desk and hugs her book often and has a deer in the headlights look when you ask her a question. Amanda says she is "stressed in history lessons," that "the lessons seem too long" and the lessons feel "difficult" and "too intense."

You remember her mother smiling and agreeing with everything you said at the last parent-teacher conference, and you are frequently not sure she knew you were trying to tell her Amanda was not doing as well as you were hoping and as her test results suggest. You know that Amanda hopes to study law and sees history as a useful subject. Amanda spends a lot of time turning around and talking to friends or silently fuming and twirling her pen. "I am almost always bored and angry . . . history lessons are almost always a waste of time," Amanda writes, and she "almost always" feels annoyed in history lessons and she always feels, she has "not accomplished anything."

Amanda is not looking forward to anything in the syllabus she says "history is worse than most subjects" but also that "history is a very important subject to study.

Martin (male, 15 Black)

"It is important "to know about your roots and where you are coming from," writes Martin. You have taught Martin the previous year, but he's still a bit of a mystery to you. He smiles and scowls easily. He sits in the middle of the room and has friends on either side of him. Your first impression of him is of a student who enjoys the work, quick to raise his hand, sometimes contributing knowledge about an obscure part of the world you know is not relevant to the lesson at hand.

Martin puts the "social" into social studies and spends much time talking and drawing. He wants to be a graphic designer and reads magazines about design when he should be working. You know he does this as you see the magazines underneath his textbook or "hidden" on his lap as he furtively glances down from time to time. At times Martin becomes very engaged and even produces extra homework you have not set. He concentrates in history lessons about "half the time" and Martin feels most involved during "the Black history part."

Martin feels distracted when studying "most European history" and strongly agreed history is an "important subject to study." But he thinks "history is worse than most subjects."

Pauline (female, 15, Black)

"When I'm learning about Black people in the time when slavery was around," this is when she feels most involved and also most alienated "when we were told about the diseases that slaves had." Pauline is the student sitting at the back in the corner of the room. She works quietly and has little to say except when the class is discussing a topic, then she lights up. In talking to her you know she wants to be "an artist and an air steward."

She likes the topics they study but does not want to continue studying history. Pauline is not sure history lessons are interesting and hardly ever concentrates during her history lessons. History, she thinks, helps her change her opinions about things. She is curious about the past, but history lessons seem too long and too remote. She likes her teacher and feels she has accomplished something of value during history. She "tended to agree" history is an important subject to study, but worse than other subjects.

What We Dislike about History Lessons
Examining the composite picture of all six students we see traces of significant issues at work in any given history lesson helping create positive or negative attitudes toward the subject and differing in importance for individual students. Both Martin and Amanda, for example, give different reasons for their dislike of history. For Amanda, of Asian descent, her perception of the difficulty of the subject is a possible reason for her saying that she feels stressed and she is not accomplishing anything of value in class. History lessons leave her feeling bored and angry.

Martin, a Black student, says he only feels involved when studying Black history. The personal feeling that he identifies is like Amanda's—"anger"—but because of the treatment of Black people in history with whom he feels a connection. His stated reason for indifference toward history lessons stems not from the difficulty of the subject but from content: "European" history bores him and Black history makes him angry.

Susan, White, and Tolu, Black, both mention specific topics they find interesting during history lessons. The topics of slavery and Nazi Germany are probably likely to be emotive for students. Susan comments on things she dislikes doing in history such as "when we do something other than answering questions, copying from the board." She thinks "reading aloud is quite good."

Tolu does not mention teaching techniques and is sure feeling interested in a lesson stems from the fact some topics are often by their very nature more interesting than others.

Loving and Loathing: Differences in Motivation
Examining the remarks of John and Pauline, there are differences in what motivates them and how they feel about the subject. For John, a White student, history is interesting because he gets to "learn about different things." He strongly agrees that history lessons are interesting and is most involved during "oral lessons" and learning in "small groups." He is alienated by his "teacher mumbling about his silly stories which mean nothing to me." In contrast, Pauline, who self-identified as Black, notes she is not sure history

lessons are interesting. She feels most involved when studying Black history but feels alienated by some of the content taught about Black people.

The remarks of these students are typical of the students taking part in the survey suggesting Black students and to a lesser extent Asian students, whether they like or dislike their history lessons is possibly linked to prior held attitudes about the importance of personal cultural content in history. Pauline and Martin think history is worse than most subjects, both agreeing they feel involved when learning about Black history.

Their feelings of involvement are, however, not necessarily based on enjoyment; Martin feels angry about the treatment of Black people. And stories about the diseases slaves suffered from leave Pauline feeling alienated. In comparison White students were more likely to comment on the teaching methods as contributory factors for feelings of engagement or them not feeling involved during history lessons.

Personal Interest
Regardless of their ethnicity students say personal interest is crucial in making what they are learning about interesting. They also write that "talking" about sensitive topics, and not being "afraid" to tackle difficult issues head on are important for them when learning history. These ideas are similar to Levstik's findings mentioned in chapter 2.

Lack of and Negative Representation
"If it was something about my religion which is Sikhism it would make lessons more interesting," says Anita (15). She emphasizes that the absence of her culture in lessons makes her "angry." Other students also insist that including more of what they consider their own histories will make school more interesting. Students answered the question "Are there times when history lessons are especially interesting? What makes this so?" Black students such as Paul wrote "When we were doing Black history, I felt annoyed and angry but much involved and interested."

Paul is a quiet thirteen-year-old boy whose grandparents settled in the country from the Caribbean in the 1950s.

Other Black students also mention anger, not because of the absence of culturally relevant material, but because of negative content concerning Black people. Nevertheless, along with the anger came engagement. Again, for Black students, slavery caused feelings of hurt, upset, and anger, but they do not mention feelings of shame as some had done in previous interviews.

Present in the survey answers is apparent pride about the survival of Black ancestors against the odds of slavery and these seem to contribute to the students not experiencing embarrassment, and it is perhaps likely that face-to-face interviews may illicit mentions of embarrassment more than paper surveys. But it is clear emotions of hurt and anger surface because some students feel a personal connection with what they perceive as negative lesson materials.

Connecting and Disconnecting:

When we were speaking about Black history I became really involved as it had something to do with me as a person. With White history there is nothing I can relate to and it is so distant and far away from me. (Joan, 14)

Joan seems highly opinionated and does not mince her words. Her mother was born in Jamaica and Joan holds strong views on what she likes learning in her history lessons. She feels involved "speaking about Black history," and her connection stems from the personal relevance she finds in the lesson's focus. She claims ownership because she can in some tangible way directly identify with what is being taught.

On the other hand, she contrasts this with how she feels during "White history." She writes that she cannot "relate to it as it is so distant and far away from me." The distance she writes of is not chronological distance; the history that they study concerning the slave trade is just as distant. However, in terms of ownership she finds difficulty connecting with what she is learning.

Answers Black students give tell us blatantly they are habitually engaged by topics that include Black people in history. However, because the roles usually assigned Black historical figures are those of people without agency, the engagement they experience is not often positive and leaves behind feelings of hurt and anger. Asian students also write about feelings of anger because of the exclusion of Asian people from the history they learn. White students also say they feel engaged by emotive topics, but their engagement is not linked to negative emotions such as anger and feeling personally hurt. Instead they become annoyed at the antics of others in the classroom.

Discussing and Understanding

Both Black and White students underscore that when allowed to discuss difficult topics, they are easier to understand, and it helps them feel more involved in what is going on in the classroom. Working in small groups makes for a deeper connection to what they are studying. Basically, they are saying what educators already know. "Telling is not teaching." When students can co-operate and interact with each other they feel more like participants and less like observers. Two of the activity's students enjoy most and which teachers may be reluctant to do or may do poorly are role-play and discussion.

Role-Play and Discussion

Using role-play and discussing issues are useful steps in getting students to think analytically; students, regardless of their writing skills, can take part. In the author's experience often the most vocally articulate students have difficulties writing fluently. Lee and Ashby (1987) discover students with learning difficulties are capable of high levels of critical thinking through verbal reasoning. Although the pupils in Lee and Ashby's research have poor reading and writing skills, their analysis of evidence can be categorized into six levels ranging from Level I, thinking that sees the past as interchangeable with the present, to Level VI where evidence is viewed in its historical context.

During subsequent interviews and surveys conducted by the author, all students (including students at college) regardless of age mention the value of discussion. It will probably not come as a surprise to any teacher that students like talking in class. Ursula (female, 14) writes, "I like Black history—I find it interesting. We had a discussion on Black history, and I enjoyed it." "When we were speaking about Black history it made me angry; that's maybe why I was so involved with the conversation." Debra (female, 14).

Once again, the issue of Black history for students of color is a source of engagement, but while one student "enjoyed" the discussion, the other suggests she felt engaged by anger. Georgia (female, 14) thinks history lessons are especially interesting "when the teacher decides to let us do some oral work, like making up plays."

Black students mention several emotions they experience during lessons about slavery such as wanting "to kill," feeling "annoyed and angry," "hurt and upset," "hatred toward White people," and being "astonished, appalled and fascinated."

Imagine, all these emotions may be bubbling and percolating as you teach.

> I felt I was really involved when we acted out a court scene. The lesson was about whether cases can be brought or changed in ways by money and if it's really up to people to decide the judgment. I felt really good because I knew what we were talking about and what we were out to see (Adiva, Asian heritage, female, 15, mother born India).

Asian students enjoyed being given the opportunity to share their ideas with their peers. This made them feel their opinions were of more value. Adiva likes feeling in control, the control you get when you understand something well. She feels a part of the lesson because she can participate fully. Feeling "good" comes from being familiar with the topic: "I knew what we were talking about." This tells you having a sense of direction, the feeling of knowing where they are going in terms of outcomes are frequently crucial for students. In the following example the climate of the classroom is what is important:

> Shirin (female, 15, mother born India): The lesson encouraged everyone in the class to join in and speak up. I felt confident and able to express myself. I felt more involved as I was communicating with members of my class.

Shirin's involvement is a result of the opportunity she has "to express" herself. Feelings of engagement come from the classroom atmosphere and the opportunity she is given to communicate her ideas and share them with other students. Interaction is a significant factor in her feeling involved during a lesson.

By contrast, Black students feel a sense of ownership and engagement during lessons about Black people in history, but the engagement is likely to be negative and alienating. Likewise, Asian students' responses also suggest involvement can stem from deep personal meanings.

> I felt involved when we were talking about Prohibition in groups discussing the advantages and disadvantages of it. I felt that it was something to argue about for health reasons, the problems it causes in , and the influence on other people. I hate people who drink. Kiki (female, 15, mother born Kenya, Asian Kenyan).

Role-play ending in purposeful discussion motivates students' interest much more directly than their working individually without interacting, because discussion is generally an open-ended activity that enables students to voice their opinions and to learn the difficult art of listening to others.

Interest and Curiosity

Like most people, students find activities interesting if they are new or they learn surprising facts about a topic they think they know. Interest and enjoyment in history lessons walk hand in hand with the curiosity factor and the teaching approach:

The teacher plays a big part in this. Theory work done at school is good. Written work at home is good. Talking and discussing topics is much more interesting than writing all lessons.

Deep-thinking student Ahimsa (female, 15, mother born Pakistan), sums up the complex nature of the issues involved in making lessons interesting and meaningful to students.

Likes and Dislikes
Surveying students highlights aspects they like and hate about history lessons. They confirm that personal relevance is an especially salient motivational aspect for them when learning. For example, Darren (male, 15, born Pakistan/mother, Kuwait) writes he did not enjoy "Greek and Roman medicine," but he felt involved in lessons about "the Middle East. I used to live in the Middle East so I was interested."

For Black students personal relevance can motivate them away from a topic as well as toward. Wendy, (female, 15, born Jamaica) says, "I felt I was switched off in the history lesson that talked about the Ku Klux Klan. I felt that those people were cruel and treated Black people bad, and for a while I felt White people needed to be revenged on. But I thought it's only history."

Another student, Rachel, (female, 14) who self-identified as Black writes, "There was a history lesson about slaves being thrown overboard on a ship. That really got to me because it was like I could feel the pain they were going through." In a sense, although these students say they are "switched off" they are very engaged.

Asian students often brought up dull routine tasks as tedious. Devi (female, 15, father born India) wrote her father's heritage (the survey only asked for birth place of mother):

> It was a more factual lesson where we were reading from sheets and taking notes. I found this lesson boring and felt tired and sleepy. The lesson was about the depression and I suppose I felt a bit depressed and bored with the subject.

Black students are often more likely to blame the topic than the teaching for feeling alienated during history lessons.

"As I said I am sick and tired about hearing about BRITISH ROYALTY AND HEROES!!!." The data indicated that for Black students a lack of references to "self" or "self-image" leads to frustration, as Joan shouts with capital letters. This issue might be linked to the idea that some cultural groups have a double historical consciousness, one that they learn at school and another that is learned from significant others. The students' responses agree with past studies such as Wineburg (2000, p. 310), who notes "children are by no means 'blank slates' when it comes to ideas and beliefs about the past."

White students also brought up a variety of topics that they found "brief and boring" including the Boston Tea Party, Leonardo Da Vinci and Richard III. Their responses indicated that the students could see no obvious personal utility in what they were studying and this nurtures their boredom.

Content and Teaching

Students of color expected a history curriculum that they could easily identify with and gain a sense of meaning for present-day living. In contrast most White students held no such anticipations. Students of color did not easily make connections between the history they were studying and themselves.

Teaching Methods and Strategies

In comparison to the seeming preoccupation of Black students with content, pedagogical methods are often the focus of White students. Teaching approaches and techniques are frequently key factors for limiting involvement for these students. Students of color do complain about teaching methods, but much less than White students. They mention a range of issues as reasons for being dissatisfied.

Dull lessons are often regularly compounded by topics that either seem irrelevant or as we have seen, when they are culturally relevant impose largely negative images of Black people on the students. Students, regardless of ethnicity, if they view school history as the memorization of names, dates, endless writing or seemingly pointless narrative, then history lessons are perhaps in danger of becoming a mindless series of exercises devoid of meaning, with little or no personal significance.

Doing History

As long ago as 1976 the Schools History Council Project challenged the idea that history is a "received subject" and argued students should be "doing history." The project also suggested the need to emphasize suitable teaching methods such as discussion as key in teaching history effectively. Shemilt's (1980) *Evaluation Study of the Schools History Project* (the project changed its name when funding ended) demonstrates that the understanding of most students learning history can be enhanced by using inquiry-based teaching methods.

Shemilt also unexpectedly discovered that the students studying project history found "greater personal relevance" in history than did the control group. This suggests students' views of the personal relevance of history may be enhanced through both rethinking the goals of school history and changing the methods in accordance with this. Of course, there is recognition that we have moved on in terms of the methodology we use and the great improvements made in textbooks. As all teachers recognize, the significance of a subject in the eyes of those on the receiving end is important.

It is interesting, but not surprising, that 76 percent of the students surveyed thought English was more important than history. Seventy-eight percent thought math was more important than history. The importance society rightly attaches to these subjects has permeated down to the thinking of students who are often able to see quickly their utility in everyday life. A failure to help students regularly make connections with what they are learning, coupled with stale teaching methods may result in the further marginality of curriculum subjects in the eyes of students at school and adults in the wider world.

Pattern of Findings

There are no easy answers as to why students become engaged and continue feeling engaged during history lessons. Broad generic complaints ran alongside more specific student concerns. For example, 60 percent of students wrote that they felt uninvolved because they did "too much reading," "too much writing," "too much listening" or watching of "videos." The issues surrounding what students think of the significance of the subject and why they feel involved are complex.

A range of reasons for becoming and staying engaged are given and students do not always follow a logical sequence in their answers. However, the following patterns emerge:

- Personal interest and enjoyment were strong motivational factors for White students choosing or not choosing to study history. Students of color are also often motivated by such feelings, but their prime motivation is personal utility.
- The majority of students said they enjoyed history lessons, (it cannot be ruled out that this might have been because they completed the survey in their history classes) but students of color are more likely to report the experience of boredom and think that history lessons are too long.
- White students are more likely to cite teaching methods over personally relevant content material and topic as a contributory factor for feelings of engagement, and feeling uninvolved during history lessons came from the antics of their peers.

- Students of color are more likely to cite personally relevant content material and topics over teaching methods as contributory factors for feelings of engagement or not feeling involved during history lessons.
- Although history is not as important as English, math, or science, the majority of students regardless of ethnicity think history is an important subject to study.
- Black students often report that they experience hurt and anger about topics that deal with Black people during their history lessons. Asian students are more likely to experience anger because of a lack of representation in the curriculum. White students are more likely to be angered by their inability to understand a concept or their dislike of a particular teaching technique.

For White students personal interest and having done well in previous years are frequently prominent factors for them choosing history as an examinable subject, as is dislike of an alternative subject option. For Black students, wanting to learn about their roots is the most important factor. Of the total group of all students 50 percent said they visited museums more than once a year. Most had watched one or two televised historical documentaries and 81 percent of all the students read historical books once or twice a year. Extra history work is not something students did willingly, although there are a few who claimed always to do extra homework.

Feelings of involvement stemmed from a complex array of factors. A key finding is that most students say history is a significant subject to study. Various reasons are given, and the most frequently mentioned are listed in the table below:

Table 5.1. Students' Reasons for Studying History

Personal Reasons	Social Reasons
To have general knowledge	Not repeating the mistakes of the past
Helps with Careers	To understand the present and the future
To learn skills	
To learn Black history	

These ideas also surfaced in the early exploratory interviews and point out that students see history in terms of social and personal purposes that range from general knowledge to understanding the present and future.

Responses from Black Students

Increasingly clear the responses from Black students included types of comments that are not generally found in the responses from White students.

Some students of color used negative emotive adjectives to describe what they thought about their history lessons such as "angry" and "appalled." White students also wrote that they became involved, but usually gave positive emotions such as "I felt good."

The responses given to the question, "Try to think of a lesson when you were really involved. What was it about the lesson that made you feel involved? How did you feel?, indicated that half of those students of color, whether or not they had chosen to study history at examination level, report they regard history as being an important subject to study. However, surprisingly some students who have been born in the country they were living in still appeared to view the history of their birth country as somewhat alien.

Fifteen Black students (63 percent) of those surveyed reported Black history as significant either in terms of wanting to know more or feeling more involved when such issues are uncovered in history lessons. Some of their comments also suggest that there is a perception that history lesson content is exclusive rather than inclusive of Black community representation.

These are complex issues. One consideration when teaching history is the argument that the way something is taught should lead the learner toward a deeper understanding of that particular area and should change the learner in some way. The range of responses to the questionnaire demonstrate that some Black students are concerned primarily with issues of meaningful content, and to a lesser extent teaching methods and strategies.

Conclusions

This chapter explored issues raised by students and gives a fuller picture of the ideas students use to make sense of the history they encounter at school and from other sources. Students' notions reveal differences in the way cultural groups react to the history they encounter at school. The issue of content is just the tip of an iceberg, and what lies hidden beneath the surface of students' statements is crucial to begin to understand the alienation of students of color from their history lessons.

In the following chapter the counterstories of older students are examined. Maturity makes them more articulate as to their thoughts concerning content.

Note

1. All names are pseudonyms.

CHAPTER SIX

Counterstories of American History
Students of Color Examine the Past

> Slavery is as equally important as any other topic in history because Black slaves are the only race of people who do not know where they come from.
>
> (Jasmine, African American)

This chapter explores the counterstories of 42 students of color in White educational spaces studying United States history. But first it gives the reader the background of how this methodology developed from directed questions that elicited answers, to getting students writing "freestyle" and choosing their own topics. Using critical race theory to summarize and frame the counterstories of students over a period of five years, the chapter focuses on the way students of color wrote, concerning historical discourses of native nations, slavery, and the American Civil War. Explored are the similarities and differences of focus within the counterstories of students of color and stories of 112 White students.

Background

The strategy of Wertsch (1994) was employed to probe the way students were thinking by the way they used written language to express ideas. Eleven undergraduates and thirty grade 11 high school students were surveyed and eight of the undergraduates were interviewed. The students interviewed did not know the author had seen their completed surveys. Students were asked to write on specific issues because this was a more focused method to begin to explore the kind of historical awareness students displayed. The exercises met certain criteria that enabled the researcher to examine how the students viewed the past, present and perhaps the future and also how their historical ideas might impact on personal and social concerns. The tasks had to be meaningful and unthreatening to students of color and White students.

The first exercise was a short extract on the life of Martin Luther King Jr., and it asked the students to say what King meant to them and their family personally and what they thought he meant to society. Later a short biography of Nelson Mandela was added. Although the use of these two men linked closely to issues of Black and White, apartheid might have influenced the responses; however, it was thought that the advantages outweighed the problems.

Task 1 Nelson Mandela
Nelson Mandela (1918–2013) was born in South Africa. In 1952 he became an African National Congress (ANC) national deputy president. Mandela advocated passive resistance to apartheid. However, after a massacre of peaceful demonstrators at Sharpesville in 1960, Mandela organized a paramilitary branch of the ANC to carry out guerilla warfare against the White government. After being acquitted in 1962 on charges of treason, he was arrested in 1964 and convicted of sabotage and sentenced to life imprisonment. A powerful symbol of the Black struggle against apartheid, Nelson Mandela was imprisoned for 27 years on a charge of conspiring to overthrow the South African Government. On his release he was named head of the African National Congress and played a leading role in organizing the first multiracial elections in April 1994. He was chosen as the first president of a free and democratically ruled South Africa. He served until 1999.

1. Does this tell you anything important for your life or your family?
2. Does this mean anything important to your society or country?

Most students did not answer the first question. These responses give you a flavor of what students Michael (White, 15) and Elizabeth (student of color, 16) wrote for both tasks:

To my life and my family "Nelson Mandela" is just a name. We know what he done, and we can just give him respect for that. By reading the extract it tells me a short version of one man's life. All I can say is knowledge is power.

It tells me that people will separate themselves because of color. It means negative things about my society and culture. It tells me my ancestors enslaved a country and held it like a prisoner for a long time. My country and society is multiracial. So, if one person's history rests on Nelson Mandela in my society, then it rests on me too as I'm a part of that society (Michael 15).

Elizabeth, like most students, did not answer the first question:

> This is very important to society. Showing the extreme of racism in the South African Apartheid, has shown people in this society/country outrageous racism by highlighting one specific case, the imprisonment of Nelson Mandela. People who do not know about the problems racism causes can see what is happening. Nelson Mandela's story was highly published in the media, which is a highly powerful source of information, informing the whole of society about the problems in South Africa (Elizabeth 16).

The second exercise using asylum seekers as a controversial issue, asked students to support two opposing views on asylum seekers.

Task 2
Write a letter to a newspaper about asylum seekers which supports the following opinion:

a. History shows that if cheap labor enters the country everyone gets worse off.

> When settlers landed in N. America they brought diseases and war with them. The Native Americans were wiped out. When settlers arrived in Africa, they enslaved it and killed any opposing forces. World War 2 showed how people with violent opinions became a danger to themselves and other people. Don't even get me started on the Middle East, always fighting and getting on each other's nerves since as long as I can remember because "so and so'" don't believe in "such and such." Religion was been the cause of more death and war than anything (Michael 15).

> Dear Editor,
> History shows that where different cultures come into contact it causes conflict in society. This was seen in 1788 when the first Europeans arrived in Australia. Aborigines were murdered and their land taken. Great conflict when two cultures met (Elizabeth 16).

Write another letter to the same newspaper about asylum seekers which supports the following opinion:

b. History shows that it is bad to treat different cultures unfairly.

> People are too rigid! Instead of looking at what's different, look at what's the same. I respect people for who they are not what they do. Everybody is different, it is that sameness in saying that "Everybody's different." Bruce Lee said "that there is conflict because people fear what they don't understand. Show them the beauty of that thing, and they no longer fear it, and it becomes a part of them" (Michael 15).

> Dear Editor,
> This can be seen at large in Britain, which is now a very multicultural society; for instance, statistics show that Indian food is Britain's most popular takeaway food. British culture has been influenced by many different cultures from around the world (Elizabeth 16).

A further revision was to use the events of World War II to gage historical consciousness of older students Maureen, White American (26) and Anita, Asian American (23):

Task 1 Second World War
The Second World War lasted for six years, from 1939 to 1945. It was a war of rapid movement and was a complex affair with major campaigns in the Pacific and the Far East, in North Africa and Russia as well as in central Europe and the Atlantic. It ended with a new kind of warfare—the atomic bomb. 50 million people died.
Please answer the following questions. You will need to write a paragraph for each question.

1. Does this tell you anything important for your life or your family? Is there any other way in which this is important?

   > THIS JUST GOES TO SHOW THAT THE PEOPLE I LOVE LIVE IN A WORLD RUN BY BASTARDS. IN THE FUTURE MY FAMILY FACES THE POSSIBLITY OF BEING MELTED INTO PAVEMENT BECAUSE THE WORLD IS RUN BY POWER-HUNGRY WHORES LIKE SADAM AND ALL THOSE OTHER CREEPY DEVILS. HOWEVER, I LIVE IN AN EVIL EMPIRE—AMERICA! THAT COUNTRY WILL EVENTUALLY BE GANGED UP ON AND MY ENTIRE FAMILY WILL BE HUNTED DOWN AND GASSED. WE LIVE IN FEAR (Maureen 26)!

This is a very concise way of summarizing the actual war. It's impossible to tell anything important of my life or my family as a result of the war and how it has shaped us in such a little space. It's short, right to the point. It does show the extent of damage and a great involvement. But it . . . (Anita 23).

2. Does this mean anything important to your society?

"Oh . . . Sure" (Maureen 26).

"I wouldn't think so. Older generations would probably be angry for the tragedy of the atomic bomb dropping to be dismissed so slightly. But again, the Japanese caused much grief among others too. This only shows figures and bare minimum facts (Anita 23).

The undergraduates completed the exercise while writing end of semester appraisals of their subjects. The high school students were given the task during a history lesson by their teacher. These exercises did elicit several responses that further demonstrated some interest and knowledge of historical issues. At the high school level students that responded demonstrated an awareness of historical matters. In the undergraduates little direct response to historical factors was shown, although a surprising level of knowledge about the problems in the Balkans was demonstrated.

The author was left wondering if the directed questions were leading some students like Maureen to not take the exercise seriously. An Asian American student Anita did respond that she thought the paragraph neglected Japan's involvement in World War II, and suffering. Interviews with eight of the undergraduates demonstrated that Maureen was worried about American involvement around the world, with Anita, the Asian American student, commenting that textbooks left out Japanese suffering when they dealt with the Second World War.

This is the background context of the counterstories in this chapter. Here students in reflections wrote concerning what they thought was significant in United States history.

Counterstories

Counterstories narrate lived encounters of racism and resistance from the perspective of marginalized people. These counterstories of the past provide insights into how students of color view and connect to the history they study and how this bifurcates into their understanding of the present (Feldman, Skoldberg & Brown, 2004). Majoritarian stories tell the dominant narrative of people with power and seem implicitly and explicitly neutral and objective. They begin with the assumption that the past may have had episodes of inequality, but everyone now enjoys equal access to the same opportunities as those that hold the reins of power.

Increasingly scholars of education have turned to narratives and the use of narrative analysis and how stories make sense and affect the way educators teach and students learn (Delgado, 1995; Boje, 2008). Exploring how students engage with their own histories and identities knowingly and unknowingly in their reflections, one glimpses their values, attitudes, and expectations. A narrative method gives agency to the unheard or muffled voices of the ordinary that may remain hidden otherwise.

By investigating stories, in the reflections of students, educators have a more complete grasp of their funds of knowledge (that is, students' ideas bring to the classroom concerning what they count as knowledge) and of them being in a certain context at a certain time (Moll et al., 1992). Clandinin and Connelly (2000, xxvi) write, "People live stories, and in the telling of these stories, reaffirm them, modify them, and create new ones."

By listening to the contours of the stories, one can grasp the cultural understanding of students being in a context at a specific time. Narrative inquiry allows you to travel "inward" to what the students may think, "outward" and "backward" and "forward" to how they connect the past with the present. Exploring students' stories "provides insights not only into what is happening but also into the understanding of the people about why and how it is happening" (Feldman, Skoldberg, and Brown, 2004, p.150).

Narrative analysis studies personal histories, which are often reflections of lived experiences and the quest for the self. Thus, the narrative has emerged as a new but central formatting device for the organization of self and identity. It frequently helps define who we are, or who we think we are, through the understanding of the stories we tell about ourselves. In this sense, the reflections actually becomes data to be analyzed and generate meaning. Narrative inquiry seeks out the problem in the narratives through the stories of people's experiences, challenges and social and cultural issues.

Czarniawska (2004) defines narrative method as one delayering grand narratives in social research, meaning simplifying the narratives for lay people. Providing an overview of the development of the narrative approach within the social sciences, Czarniawska's *Narratives in Social Science Research* emphasizes the importance of narratives for the qualitative researchers who want to investigate new vistas. Czarniawska (2004) defines narrative methods as a "naturalistic genre" (p. viiii) since it has to do with many aspects and forms of everyday life. She writes that the "raw world was lived and experienced by its subject" (p. viiii).

Czarniawska (2004) writes of how stories are often made, collected, provoked, interpreted, analyzed, deconstructed, put together, and set against/together with other stories. If we restrict research to the use of only data and facts, we cannot address the multiple social complexities in different cultural contexts that researchers have to contend with. The narrative method enables researchers to unearth aspects that hard-core science might have forgotten or left untouched.

Silent Observers

The author, observing students over the past decade in places of learning in mainly White southern educational spaces, noted the engagement of African Americans, Latinos/as and Asian Americans tended to fall into the category of silent observers, seldom asking questions, only speaking directly if asked a direct question, and joining in discussions when prompted, but falling mute when issues of race and immigration arose. Levstik (2000) makes similar observations. Furthermore, although silent in classrooms, students of color vividly expressed ideas in their writing, and passionately asked numerous questions.

The unbridled flow of funds of knowledge in the work of multicultural students awakened a desire to better understand their historical consciousness in terms of what they were focusing on in United States history (Rüsen, 2004). Educators recognize that understanding prior knowledge of students enables teachers to make more targeted choices about how and what they teach from a place of more comprehensive knowledge (Weber, 1990; Millis and Cottell, 1998).

The self is structured in language. A person's history, hopes and dreams are said to be systematized and shaped in language in a narrative form (Burr, 2003). Therefore, using a narrative method is central to exploring the way students construct and understand dominant historical narratives and alternative histories, and the way students "think the world." Reading their counterstories we are commonly able to grapple with the way they socially construct their ideas and histories and why alternative histories are regularly important. By carefully considering their metaphors, grammatical constructions, figures of speech and so on, we get a clearer picture of the way they probably construct their stories.

Setting and Participants

This study took place over a period of five years and is focused on undergraduate students taking a general education prerequisite United States history course with the same teacher at Essendine,[1] a mainly White four-year college situated in the southern United States. The course explored major themes in North American history from pre-Columbus in the United States to 1900.

Teacher instruction was comprised of a mixture of methods and strategies ranging from problem solving in history, evaluating primary and secondary sources, interactive lectures, and a variety of collaborative learning techniques. Most students (if schooled in the United States) had covered content aspects of the course, albeit probably at an introductory level during their previous education experiences. In survey courses, a measure of disconnectedness from students jaundiced regarding another foray into what some conflate as, the Columbus Exchange, Revolution and Civil War is often expected. The table below details cultural composition years 1–5[2]:

Table 6.1. Students in Study

Number of students in study	Opting out	Students in study
Students of color	2	42
White students	11	112
Total	13	154

Research Questions

Collecting data in the form of students' reflections took place during the last week of each semester. Students were formally asked to complete a consent form which gave permission to use research data. They received promises of anonymity and could choose to opt out.

They were given the following instructions:

Choose two topics that you have studied in this course that you think are historically significant and reflect on and evaluate them in terms of how important they are to American history.

An attempt was made to answer the following research questions:

- Which aspects of U.S. history do students of color think significant?
- Which aspects of U.S. history do White students think significant?

- A subsidiary question was: Do the ways students of color think about similar U.S. history topics differ from White students?

This discussion focuses on three common themes emerging from the reflections: Native Nations, slavery, and the Civil War.

Counterstories of Native Nations: Students of Color

Both students of color and White students wrote regarding the treatment of Native Nations. The data revealed that twelve female students focused on Native Nations as significant in United States history. No male students wrote concerning Native Nations as significant. Six non-White students wrote regarding Native Nations, four Asian Americans and two African Americans. The comments here give a flavor of how non-White students rewrote the history they had learned:

> When I study America and its beginnings, I learn about the heroic endeavors of the settlers, the dreadful trials they suffered, and the greatness they achieved. . . . I would consider the arrival of White settlers and the exchanges to be an unparalleled catastrophe that brought about an "American Holocaust" (Jennifer,[3] Asian American, female).

Jennifer pushes past deficit narratives she may have learned regarding the early colonization of the New World and her views when evaluating the events and the outcomes for Native Nations. She learned apropos the "heroic" deeds of the early settlers. She does not use language that suggests a strong attachment to American history.

Her comments strongly indicate that history lessons have focused on the "dreadful trials" of the White colonists juxtaposed with "the greatness they achieved." Jennifer's story passes judgment on colonization, calling it "an American Holocaust." In similar fashion Pauline, an African American student, tells a story of the Columbus exchange, which for her is critical in understanding the repercussions on generations later in the contemporary world.

> Before the Europeans came to the Americas, the natives prospered and had not been exposed to diseases like influenza, measles and typhus, and smallpox, or alcohol. The Europeans came and took the land that they had flourished on and left the natives with a small corner of a large continent. To this day the effects of European colonists are still seen in Native American society. They have been placed on reserves, many of them suffer from severe alcoholism and

Native Americans have the highest suicide rate of all ethnic groups (Pauline, African American, female).

Pauline does not use pronouns to indicate that she feels some sense of ownership or belonging to the history she is learning. She uses the words "native" and "Native Americans" to describe indigenous peoples. Pauline's story does not mention anything positive coming out of the Columbian Exchange for Native Nations. "Before the Europeans came . . . the Natives prospered . . . the effects of European colonists are still seen. . . . severe alcoholism . . . highest suicide rate of all ethnic groups." This is a damming indictment of the Columbus Exchange.

Their textbooks, readings and lectures had considered the positive aspects of the Columbus Exchange, but all six non-White student stories focused on the calamity wrought on the Native Nations as being more important than any good coming from the bargain.

All the students of color went further in passing judgment, and attributing blame, some also hinting that what happened to Native Nations was indicative of "White society." Commenting on "a moral code of 'White' society" Shilpa, a self-identified Asian American, tells a story which judges the actions of Whites and their treatment of Native Nations as "shamefully interesting" and "ironic" that "amateurs in the New World thought they knew better than the people that lived there."

Shilpa's counterstory is of the negative actions of "Christians" toward non-Christians using "help" as a destructive feature of their goal of native "assimilation." She enlarges her story to include "White" society of today, and her use of the words "it has been" suggests that she still thinks this is an ongoing sentiment of "White" society:

> It has been a moral code of the "White" society to try to help those who are not of Christian faith or said "heathens" by making the natives more like them. I have found this theory shamefully interesting. . . . I have always found it ironic how Englishmen declared the natives "savages" and in need of assimilation into a society of a merciful god when the Englishmen were amateurs in the New World. (Shilpa, Asian American female)

Shilpa distances herself from this history and uses it to understand the contemporary world. It teaches her a lesson that is "ironic" and "shameful."

White Students and Native Nations

White students' stories in general take on the tone of majority histories regarding Native Nations, using words which are frequently much more lenient and matter of fact than non-White students. Daisy wrote:

> The unfortunate tragedy of the Trail of Tears. . . . we know that in actuality the Indians were driven by force from their lands and the older history books had a way of distorting history, so one must be cautious, in what they read and how the information is interpreted. (Daisy, White American Female)

In her story the Trail of Tears is "unfortunate" and there is an acknowledgment that "the Indians were driven by force," but, she makes no value judgment apropos this action, although she does use the word "force" and comments on "older history books distorting the past." This may reference class assignments exploring the way different history textbooks portrayed events. She continues, "so one must be cautious, in what they read and how the information is interpreted." Daisy deftly moves from a statement of fact to the skill of treating historical sources with informed skepticism. The use of "we" suggests ownership of what she is learning.

Another student's story has similar tones:

> Even though forcing the Indians out of their homes . . . are not our proudest moments as Americans, it is a crucial part of our history and it is important to recognize its occurrence. Every country, just like every person, has faults and a past. But the important thing is to grow and learn from them. (Christy, White American, female)

In Christy's story the treatment of Native Nations as "not our proudest moment" suggests ownership and a measure of responsibility toward the history. She writes regarding the treatment of Native Nations as "a crucial part of our history" and her judgment is diffused through the lens of "every country." America is not unique in having done things that are in hindsight questionable. Christy then likens the mistreatment of Native Nations further, not only to "every country" but "every person has faults and a past." She does not dwell on the negative aspects, but for her "the important thing is to grow and learn from them." Christy probably wants to move on, to learn the lesson and "grow."

Laura's story:

> Events like the Black Hawk War and *Cherokee Nation v. Georgia* show the intelligence and resistance within the Indian people. . . . I always understood the brutality of the Trail of Tears; however, I always viewed the Indians almost as outsiders. . . . knowing the Indians knew their rights according to the Constitution . . . leads me to be more inclusive. (Laura, White American, female)

Laura writes that she "always understood the brutality of the Trail of Tears" but the topic of the "Black Hawk War and *Cherokee Nation v. Georgia*" made her more accepting of "the intelligence and resistance within the Indian people." She writes "I always viewed the Indians almost as outsiders." In Laura's story the use of American courts by Native Americans and that they knew their constitutional rights, makes her think of them in a more "inclusive" light. Laura recognizes the "brutality" and the yardstick she uses to measure Native Nations is their use of European tools to try to resist White American actions. This shows the intelligence of Native Nations who now perhaps seem to appear less like "outsiders" in her thinking.

Seeing Native Nations as outsiders contrasts with the stories of students of color who wrote of Whites as outsiders or "amateurs'" in the New World. Other students' stories underscored their scant knowledge of Native American histories:

> One surprising thing about education reform was that people were teaching American Indians. They believed they could be "civilized" if they were taught how to behave and act and the traditions of the White world. (Amanda, White American, female)

Amanda's story focuses on being surprised that "American Indians . . . were taught how to behave and act and the traditions of the "White world." Her story is one of surprise and by placing the word "civilized" in inverted commas she is voicing her unease at the word and shows detachment from the history by not using personal pronouns. Nevertheless, when we compare her comment to Shilpa's comment, (although not concerning the same event) "I have found this theory shamefully interesting," there is a contrast between the outright condemnations of Shilpa in comparison with Amanda who is "'surprised."

In Shilpa's story she is not surprised; in her stated experience it is a natural part of "a moral code of White society and shameful."

Counterstories of Slavery: Students of Color

Unsurprisingly, the stories of students of color, especially those of African Americans writing on slavery, differed in intensity and focus from White students. Only one White student in five years wrote about slave resistance, and only four African Americans focused on the way African Americans coped with enslavement. Devon, a student of African American descent, encapsulates the flavor in his story:

> slaves came together and made the best of what they had . . . most slaves cultivated their own Negro spirituals. . . . Religion, language and music are the most cultural adaptations that slaves evolved and made their own (Devon, African American, male).

In his story "slaves came together" and they used what they had to survive and thrive. Although materially they had little, they did adapt and make their "own negro spirituals. . . . Religion, language" they adapted and syncretized and made new things that became their own.

Most African American students concentrated on owning the personally harrowing aspects of slavery and racism:

> The topic of slavery impacts my feelings so much because I grew up in the South; I have witnessed racism that continues to live on through years by people who are unfortunately ignorant of what colored people still experience to this day (Faith, African American, female).

For Faith her story is probably not just something impersonal from the textbook but part of a lived experience. This story is personal and it "impacts my feelings"; it is a lived experience having a deep resonance in that she "grew up in the South." She makes direct links from slavery to microaggressions of daily life (Pierce, 1970). Whether these are often conscious or done on purpose the story does not elaborate, but for Faith these are probably frequently actions that trigger an emotional reaction. "I have witnessed racism that continues to live on . . . colored people still experience to this day." Interestingly she uses the term "colored people" which is either inclusive of all people of color or a throwback to a pre–civil rights term that some southern White Americans still use.

Faith's counterstory blames the "ignorance" of "people" unaware that microinsults and micro invalidations are probably a daily routine in the lives of many people of color (Sue, et al., 2007). Fascinatingly, in her story she has "witnessed racism" but, she does not say she has been on the receiving end. However, this witnessing of "daily" racism leads her to "feel" strongly concerning the topic. Had she not experienced racism, or if she had, is she distancing herself? It is not clear from her story. For other students of color the issue of slavery was one of a lost sense of identity and the status that majoritarian history gives to the topic is refuted:

> Slavery is as equally important as any other topic in history because Black slaves are the only race of people who do not know where they come from and what their nationality is (Jasmine, African American, female).

Jasmine's counterstory suggests slavery is viewed as less important than other historical storylines she has grown up with. The pedigree of slavery in her opinion is "equally important as any other topic." She writes, "Black slaves" are a "race of people" that do not know their history. They have had their knowledge of where they came from and "their nationality" stripped from them. Stating Black enslaved people are the "only" people that have this forced amnesia suggests Jasmine has strongly held views.

Her story also includes ideas of a lost historical identity and imposed identity when she asks the following, "Negro means Black which is a color, not a race and Africa is a continent so why are we called African American?" Here is a question she wants an answer to. By using the pronoun "we" Jasmine shows personal ownership. She also implies the term "American" is the reserve of White Americans, her story perhaps suggesting White Americans are not generally referred to as White Americans. Furthermore, the storyline calls into question the habitually acceptable error of seeing Africa as a country. In this she implies historical amnesia and imposed identities leave her with many unanswered questions.

Other non-White students linked slavery with other historical issues and time periods:

> I still question the colonists because the belief of life and liberty and the ability to be represented did not fall to all men. Colonists did not like the feeling of oppression ordained by an outside source. So what makes it okay that slavery exists even in those times . . .? The idea that all men are created equal did not include all men. Minorities, women, children had no rights. . . . The truth is that slaves were neither considered human beings nor creatures with feelings. They were viewed as nothing more than property to their owners. (Scarlet, Latina American, female)

Scarlet's counterstory challenges ideas of "life and liberty and the ability to be represented." Her story questions why during the Revolutionary period, a time of freedom, slavery prospered. She uses no personal pronouns to show ownership or a sense of belonging. Her story points out the irony of the patriot cause and points out that the "all men are created equal" mantra was exclusionary. Scarlet's story uses the word "minorities" for people absent from "life, liberty and the pursuit of happiness." She also answers the question that she poses. "Slaves were neither considered human beings nor creatures with feelings." In Scarlet's counterstory it was beyond the thinking of patriots to view "minorities" as anything more than inanimate property.

White Students and Slavery

In their stories White students seldom wrote concerning the issue of slavery. When the "peculiar institution" was mentioned it was in conjunction with other aspects of American history and not the focus of their stories. For example, Adam's story concerns the "revolutionary" nature of the cotton gin and he does mention "the practice of African American slavery":

> In 1793 Eli Whitney invented the cotton gin. A revolutionary invention in its day, the cotton gin not only increased productivity, but rekindled and ensured the practice of African American slavery across the southern states (Adam White American, male).

Unlike the stories of students of color, no comments are made as to the moral virtues or lack thereof of slavery, just a statement of fact that the cotton gin "rekindled and ensured the practice of African American slavery." This story is measured in tone, is void of emotion or value judgment and is what history teachers often demand when students are writing papers. Another student, Nate, wrote that "the single most troubling aspect of pre–Civil War America is the complete inability of our national leaders to adequately deal with the issue of African-American slavery."

Nate's story indicates personal feeling by saying the issue is "most troubling." This suggests disquiet, but, perhaps understandably it does not have the raw emotion that students of color attach to the topic when they write. White students that did write stories about the topic often mentioned their lack of prior knowledge concerning slavery. Their stories demonstrate many probably found the issue challenging:

> Slavery brought another kind of human race across the world into the United States and expanded our knowledge to new cultures. Slavery was horrible, but it expanded the imports and exports that go through the United States because

slaves did the work and helped produce these products long ago (Leanne, White American, female).

In Leanne's story slavery was "horrible" but the positive side of slavery was the expansion of knowledge gained from cultures meeting each other. Her use of the words "another kind of human race" is clumsy and disquieting. Leanne's story may suggest that slavery was a necessary evil; it "expanded the imports and exports that go through the United States." Three White students in five years wrote reflections that condemned slavery outright.

In Jane's story, which refutes majoritarian stories, she asks questions and links the past to the present and clearly makes value judgments linked to the present:

> What made them think it was okay to take a person, claim them as property, and then use them like an expendable tool . . . when is it going to end? What is (it) going to take for people to start treating other people *like people*? (Jane, White American, female).

Jane distances herself from the history using the word "them" and she, much like the students of color, asks questions not of "Why" but of "What" and "When."

Most White students wrote stories regarding their ignorance of aspects of slavery:

> I did not know that slaves were sold at auction just like cattle. . . . I did not know that slavery was on the decline until the cotton gin was invented. . . . (Fugitive Slave law)I did not know this law was put into effect and I thought once slaves got to the North they were free (Terri, White American, female).
>
> I was not aware of the intensity of slavery and how life for slaves was so extremely difficult and inhumane . . . I learned that despite how hard slaves worked for their owners, they were still seen as lazy (Brianna, White American, female).

In summary of this section students of color asked "Why" questions concerning slavery coupled with its contemporary influences in their counter-stories, suggesting they were not getting answered in ways that adequately met their needs. White students' stories overwhelmingly expressed statements of "I didn't know," suggesting they had probably never been taught regarding the harsher realities of the slave trade.

The Civil War

The Civil War was a topic students of color were silent on. White students wrote copious stories regarding the war. This is not surprising, for educational spaces in the American South are surrounded with monuments and events commemorating the war, and where many personal connections are probably very much intact. However, they never wrote about the causes of the war, but individual battles, events and leaders were almost always present in their stories.

> I pictured what June 27, 1864 must have looked like with William T. Sherman's union forces from Atlanta. Bodies were everywhere with casualties estimated around 4,000 (Confederates 1,000 and Union 3,000). The two armies seemed to be playing a gory game separated by the small chain of mountains (Bonnie, White American, female).

Bonnie's story details the enormous casualties that the war inflicted on the South during Sherman's march, contrasted with the scenic beauty of where it occurred. For her this is vivid and "a gory game."

Other White students explicitly said that the causes of the war did not interest them, "One of the most interesting times of American history in my opinion is the Civil War and not specifically why it was fought, but more how it was fought" (Austin, White American, male).

Other stories praised people that fought for the Confederate cause:

> I learned the Confederate army was comprised of all types of men, from older parents to young teenagers. I had the utmost respect for the older men who went. I thought it was commendable that they loved their way of life so much that they were willing to risk their lives to try to save it (Bo, White American, male).

Bo has "the utmost respect for the older men who went"; furthermore he finds it "commendable" that they were fighting to preserve "their way of life." The value judgments that Bo's story makes are perhaps that it was an honorable endeavor and a just cause. His use of the words "utmost respect" and "commendable" suggests ownership of the history. In essence Bo probably seems to see nothing wrong in fighting for the right of what students of color may well view in essence as "White supremacy."

Bo may possibly have been taught publicly and privately that the war was about state's rights and the right to own enslaved people was a minor byproduct of the war.

Students of Color and White Students' Counterstories of Post–Civil War Life

Three students of color wrote regarding the aftermath of the Civil War and their own personal connections to post–Civil War life, recounting stories heard from relatives:

> Picking cotton and the cotton gin is something I am quite familiar with. My grandfather and mother often told me stories of how they picked cotton all day long. . . . My grandfather was paid by the pound and not the hour, so you had to work really hard to get a few pounds. . . . They had to feed and support their families and cotton picking was a major employer of Blacks even after slavery ended (John, African American, male).

The practice of share-cropping for many African Americans in the South is something they have a familial connection with. For White students many have strong familial attachments to mill work. In her reflection Alice wrote about why she thought the cotton gin was significant:

> I found this topic of interest because the cotton industry is connected to me for the reason that both of my grandfathers, most of my aunts and uncles and their children all in the same southern town work at the same cotton mill. . . . I found it fascinating how this entire town can revolve around one industry" (Alice, White American, female).

It is the personal connection and personal knowledge that allow these students to claim ownership of the history, and makes the cotton gin of interest to the student of color, whose ancestors harvested the cotton, and to the White student whose ancestors worked in cotton mills, a major hub of post–Civil War Southern industry.

Discussion

Jörn Rüsen's, (1993) typology for historical consciousness is a helpful tool for trying to find explanations as to why the counterstories of students of color focused so much on criticizing majoritarian stories of the past, and questioned the treatment of people, but seldom was this done by White students. Rüsen's suggestion of four key categories in understanding how historical consciousness operates is a useful starting point for trying to unpack why the students focused on aspects of American history that were unpalatable and they thought seeped into the present. The categories developed by Rüsen are

- "Traditional" category. This sees the past in terms of a "binding obligation" to protect the ties that link us to the past.
- "Exemplary" category. The past is seen in terms of providing "general principles," rules that give guidance to the way we function in the present.
- "Critical" category. The past is not binding on the present and messages and actions of the past are critically scrutinized.
- "Genetic" category. This category recognizes that change is central to the historical process and that the passing of time changes identities. Identity is not a static entity but is transformed by change, and survives by change, as well as evolving through it (Rüsen, 1993, p. 64).

Rüsen does not view these categories as discrete and separate in the minds of people. He suggests that they overlap, and individuals do not exclusively use one type of historical consciousness but switch between categories. If the findings of this study are interrogated using Rüsen's typology, the evidence indicates (as suggested by Rüsen) that the students of color and White students do not individually use only one type of historical consciousness exclusively but change when discussing different aspects of history.

Students of color tended to fall into the third category when they used stories critical of events such as Jennifer when she wrote, "I would consider the arrival of White settlers and the exchanges to be an unparalleled catastrophe that brought about an "American Holocaust." They also used the first category when talking of links with themselves and ancestors of the past. White students tended to use the genetic category. For them their identities were not unchangingly linked to the harsh aspects of the past. For example, Christy said, "Every country, just like every person, has faults and a past. But the important thing is to grow and learn from them." They also used traditional modes of protecting ties that link them to the past, particularly in using personal pronouns when discussing aspects of the past.

Although the theory is a useful tool in trying to decipher why students of color focused on harsh aspects of United States history in their stories, it is treated with an equal measure of interest and caution.

Increasingly, scholars of education have turned to narratives and the use of narrative analysis. They explore how stories make sense and affect the way educators teach and students learn, enabling educators to envisage, inspire, and make changes in education. Practitioner research can be a powerful tool in the arsenal of educators. Looking at the way students of different heritages engage with their own identities knowingly and unknowingly in their accounts, you get a glimpse into their values, attitudes and to some extent their expectations about history.

Because the sample is small, generalizations cannot be made, but the findings help point out specific issues students of color frequently think are significant when they are learning United States history. In their comments, all students sift through a range of challenges and curiosities they find intriguing or want answers too. History is a discipline driven by questions, and a subject which can help answer some students' queries concerning the present and perhaps the future. However, it was clear these students' questions concerning race and racism in the past and present were not being answered. Nor perhaps can history ever do so. In the United States race is a significant mediating factor for students of color; therefore, unsurprisingly, students of color had the most questions around issues of slavery and racism.

The main question students of color wanted an adequate answer for was, why was the acceptance of slavery in the past and racism today so normal in American society? For example, in this student's story, "so why did so many others feel that African Americans did not deserve to live equally in society? (Veronica, African American, female)." The idea that freedom was something you must "deserve" and not inalienable rankles with her. Commenting on the view of Robert Tombs that American Slavery was a "desirable good," in this student's story she questions his claim by asking what he used as comparison to reach his conclusion, "Robert Tombs stated that the South had a "mild and humane" society with fewer than 800,000 slaves. This may be true but in comparison to what? (Sonia, African American, female). A question that Faith asks is repeated often in the reflections from students of color:

> The question I would like to know would be "when will racism end"? Although that is a question I wish I could write about, unfortunately I do not have an answer (Faith, African American, female).

Educators too have no clear answer to this question. Nevertheless, giving students an opportunity to talk about the history of racism entwined in attitudes and actions of the past, and the way this has left indelible fingerprints on the present that probably stretch into the future makes it an issue that educators should confront.

Students were given the opportunity to write a reflection about a historical site. They could choose the site, but it had to be linked to America after 1890 to the present. Many chose to visit a Civil Rights Center. Students wrote that what started out as fulfilling a class requirement turned into something that made them examine aspects of life many took for granted:

This museum has a major impact on everyone who walks into it and illustrates the pain and fight for equal rights for African Americans and people around the world. It is important that people go and visit this site not only just to say they have been there but to gain knowledge and respect for the people that were involved and led the Civil Rights Movement. . . . It is important for Black and White children to go and learn about the civil rights so that they never forget how much their ancestors went through just so they could sit next to one another in class (Male White American).

Studies prove students learn best when they are habitually actively engaged in their learning experiences, be they from formal study or direct observation (Nager & Shapiro, 2007). And when teaching controversial issues, it is possible for a lesson to degenerate into a "hierarchy of oppression" of who suffered most in history instead of getting students to understand concepts such as "equivalent" (Ladson-Billings, 2000).

One of the most uncomfortable parts of United States history is the issue of slavery, which is still a difficult subject. A few years ago, a children's book "A birthday cake for George Washington" created a storm of protest and was withdrawn from publication over its "superficial" portrayal of slavery (*New York Times* January 17, 2016, p. B6).

In the state of Georgia, not for the first or last time, a teacher's chosen method to teach about slavery met with strong criticism from some parents (*Atlantic Journal Constitution* August 13, 2016). So, educators cannot be reckless in the approaches and strategies they use to confront these emotive issues. Nor can they turn teaching into "Heroes and Holidays" when just digging a little deeper into the master narratives often uncovers layers of ignored or forgotten histories which can enrich the classroom experience of all students, and help them question and answer some of the "why" questions they have concerning "the structural inequality, the racism, and the injustice that exist in society" today (Ladson-Billings, 1994, p. 128).

Notes

1. Pseudonyms are used for all the names of research participants and locations.
2. As the numbers of minority students were small, years were numbered 1–5 for anonymity.
3. All student names are pseudonyms

CHAPTER SEVEN

An Approach for Teaching World History

> As a minority student born in another country, I could not identify myself in the learning and I never really got to see different perspectives other than our "western ideology."
>
> (male, Latino heritage)

This chapter explores the use of literature as a resource for teaching world history. It quarries beneath the surface of a history education offering as a prerequisite for preservice teachers. Focusing on difficult questions and perspectives, the chapter uncovers how a critical pragmatism approach to learning and teaching world history can pay dividends in helping students engage with inner invisible understandings concerning personal identities, enabling them to sift through cultural, racial, religious, and class diversity in a non-threatening and productive manner (Richert and et al, 2009).

Here students' self-reported ideas, perceptions, and the experience of the class with reference to assigned literature from reflections over a period of three years are examined. In years one and two the texts read were Umberto Eco's *Baudolino* and Robert B. Marks's *The Origins of the Modern World*. Burke, Christian, and Dunn's *World History for Us All: The Big Eras: A Compact History of Humankind for Teachers and Students*, was included in year three.

The approach of using a novel, a textbook and a history text with an alternative narrative concerning the origins of the modern world aims to help students uncover and recognize their own cultures and how a person's culture influences their understanding of the world and its history. The course strives to make students more aware of the workings of the discipline and that the way history is made, and understood, is also a product of culture.

This gives a deeper understanding of how culture determines approaches to history. If students are frequently better able to understand how and why they interpret historical events and experiences in the way they do, they are probably more likely to recognize and be more accepting of alternative interpretations when they meet them, or need to use them, in and outside of the classroom. Narrative analysis points out the flaws and gaps in the way we teach and learn and experience history. Narrative analysis helps us find alternatives to cultural biases, oppressive power relationships, and dominating epistemologies.

The narrative analysis of the texts students engage in helps them find what the stories imply through the discovery of how logic is made and how they use "syllogism" in understanding history and the teaching of history as a discipline. The narrative analysis of the students' stories about the stories they read coupled with the educator's own experience aids in seeing how they make their logic and how both educator and students use "'syllogism" to make sense of experiences. Feldman, Skoldberg, and Brown (2004) write about syllogism analysis to "find logics that run across many different stories and to show how narratives construct archetypical characters that are simplistic representations" (p.167).

Thus, narratives should be in the arsenals of those that construct educational policy and with those of us directly involved in interacting with preservice teachers because trainers of teachers draw conclusions about preservice teacher education based on the "assumptions about characters that are often implicit in 'stories'" (Feldman, Skoldberg, and Brown, 2004, p.167). First and foremost, narrative method values "experience." Experience and personal stories give voice to the unheard or muffled voices of the students you teach and to some extent to educator practitioners.

Participants

There were eighty-eight participants, and thirty-eight were female and fifty male. They were all either declared history or history-education interest students. The researcher did not ask for demographic details, but some students in their writing did self-report individual heritage.

Context

The class was a prerequisite for entry into a history education program. Five cohorts spanning three years were examined. Each class met twice weekly for two hours a day. Each week one class was devoted to literature analysis and discussion, the other class to teaching strategies and methods.

Baudolino, Fantasy, or the Lying Historian

It is an anathema for many who teach a subject whose basis is "truth" to use a lying historian to show the necessity of searching for truth. However, this is not giving the intelligence of would-be history teachers enough credit. The study of fictions and fictional biographies alongside more traditional historical texts helps students recognize the flaws and truth in seemingly "perfect" narratives. Studying and reflecting on the characters they meet and seeing how they highlight the paradoxes found in society that are usually not reflected in the dominant narrative to which they are accustomed enables them to deconstruct the historical images of "self" or "us" and reconstruct "other" or "them."

The focus of the class is not the incorrect aspects of the lying historian's work. When reading Umberto Eco's novel, future teachers gain an appreciation of Umberto Eco's mastery of the written word, his encyclopedic knowledge of medieval White mythology, and the serious nature of teaching the discipline.

The daunting task of tackling *Baudolino* is mirrored in the undertaking of fostering in these students a deeper understanding of intercultural competence, and comprehensive awareness of competing historical narratives. Both are often crucial prerequisites because of the changing demographic landscapes of classrooms in the United States. Helping students to correctly identify and frame challenges with the theoretical underpinnings of history as a discipline is one task. Along with this, students need to use research-based ideas to answer questions, and practices and strategies to serve the needs of different cultures they will undoubtedly meet in schools.

The capstone of the course is to plan and teach a world history lesson using the standards of their state, and what they have learned over the semester, to their peers who critique and evaluate each lesson by providing written feedback on the process and ideas used by their peers and themselves.

Baudolino is not an easy read. Some students loved the "lying historian" immediately, and for others it was a book they learned to respect. At 521 pages it is lengthy and begins with the child protagonist Baudolino defacing a manuscript in order to write his own history. Written in rudimentary Latin, the beginnings of the story are a hurdle for some students, but once they have jumped into the events they are frequently quickly engaged. Seeing Baudolino acting in this cavalier way throughout the book, and having students ask each other targeted "why" questions, they become more skilled at recognizing how historical events can be distorted, or that "fake news" and fabricated histories need an element of believability about them and a naïve or self-deluded audience to be successful.

One learning goal is to help students relate to what they are reading personally and the possible impact in a classroom. Students are asked in their reading and discussions to say what they find interesting in each chapter and to think about and relate personal experiences to increase their understanding. One result is that students better understand that the White American tradition of constructing history is a linear process. They are regularly forced by personal experiences to acknowledge White American culture gives great weight to physical evidence as a way of explaining human behavior.

Helping preservice teachers recognize why history educators prod students to focus on historical understanding and disciplined inquiry is clearly seen in *Baudolino*. This enables students to uncover what this actually means, and most importantly what it does not mean in practice and the dire consequences if ignored.

Eco's historical knowledge can be daunting for students, who easily grasp one of the main issues they will often meet when teaching world history, namely the vastness of the subject. Through the antics of the main protagonist students wrote they realized the importance of strong content knowledge, and the central value of reliable sources. Also, they said it gave them a deeper understanding of how counterfactual histories work, and the possibility that the historical past may be distorted or may have been different with just the tweak of a fertile imagination.

In numerous ways the book *Baudolino* also challenges students to tackle issues of identity, cultural divisions, class and religious affiliations, and world-views that may influence how they see and experience the people around them, and probably the way they have learned and will often teach history. Students talk about potential triggers, hot button topics and issues such as the racial microaggressions and subtle words that trigger emotionally reactions. These include and are not limited to microassaults done with intention and for a particular purpose—for example, racial name calling and actions which are racially discriminatory. Microinsults often implicitly infer inferiority and a masked insulting message. Microinvalidations are prominent in dominant histories where they negate the lived lives of students of color and are often masked by claims by those offending as color blindness.

Particularly in the study of history the reality of school diversity brings with it issues of invisible internal forces such as identity, ownership, and belonging that teachers and students carry internally. Helping students to assess their own triggers and topics they find disconcerting is established in a nonthreatening manner as they bring the topics up themselves in their discussions. These matters, like most of the cultural iceberg, lie hidden in plain sight (Hall, 1977). For educators helping all students fulfil their potentialities is daunting, and making sure they pay attention to the triggers that they may consciously notice in themselves, but be unaware of in their students, is critical.

Aspects of history learned in the classroom will almost certainly "push some buttons" and students may silently withdraw, feel powerless and have a sense of apathy or hostility and anger. Helping educators increase their awareness of such issues and how to avoid engaging in microaggressions and counteract them is crucial.

Part of what makes *Baudolino* so engaging and useful is that it shows just how "messy" and complex history is. Textbooks are likely to give students the idea that "this happened, and then that," a clean linear storyline. Eco's dealings with writing history, stereotyping, and religious differences prod students to unravel their own perceptions and misconceptions. They analyze perspectives, and are often prompted to make connections and acknowledge inner invisible cognitive responses that they probably would not make through the reading of most history textbooks.

Such connections include acknowledging in a classroom setting that some students will often dominate conversations, and the way this happens varies between cultures. Teaching preservice teachers to recognize this in their own groups and how it may happen in a classroom setting is key to facilitating thoughtful targeted discussions. Students learn to share discussion space with each other and how to do this in the classroom with students from different cultures.

Employing narrative analysis to the reflections of students helps find the implicit in their narrative voices and this aids in exposing counterstories that are commonly useful for educators as they grapple with refining the history teaching. This creates a situation in which meaning is made through "binary opposition" (Miller, 2012; Feldman, Skoldberg, and Brown, 2004). For example, when looking at the role of the "invisible hand" of historians in historical narratives, students create alternative meanings of what a historian is from what a historian is not. Viewing narrative in the post-modern context is a tool through which the meaning is made through the practice of binary opposition. Students uncover cultural biases, oppressive power relationships, and dominating epistemologies that guide them into seeing the implicit that grand historical narratives neglect to accentuate.

Narrative analysis is therefore crucial for the educator and students to better understand alternative narratives and how they may give great depth to their teaching of the world. In the course of emphasizing the importance of narrative inquiry, Griffiths and Macleod (2008) write that anecdotes can affect strategies. They write in the context of changing policy through anecdotes: "Anecdotes told to powerful people may change their minds about issues, where other sources of information and argument have not" (p.125) and they see much truth and validity in the narrative. In this regard, it seems crucial for educators to use the narratives of our students as we design and redesign our courses, in particular the narratives of our underrepresented student groups. Griffiths and Macleod (2008) write:

> There frequently are some areas of study to which auto/biographical research can be seen as being particularly well suited. First, the experience of people at the margins, such as those whose lives intersect more than one dimension of difference such as race, class, gender, disability, or sexuality. Narrative research has been presented as a method for giving a stage to the voices of people who traditionally have had not been heard. (p.137)

In this regard critical theory plays a synergistic role in identifying the oppression of the marginalized and enabling their voices to be heard. The author's research has always looked to the narratives of marginal groups through interviews and personal reflections. Here she concentrates on the reflections as part of narrative inquiry because the study of auto/biographies is very important to recognize the unspoken and buried meanings.

Narratives are a means to investigate human experience, and they are often the formations of the here and now (Bruner, 1991). When you analyze narrative reality, you give "narrative form" to experience (Gubrium & Holstein, 2009), and narrative analysis uncovers a sense of what happened or what might happen. In the postmodern condition (Lyotard, 1984), narratives fashion meaning in open and collaborative situations. When narratives, in this case reflections, are made, they are made first and foremost to make sense for themselves, to make a meaning of the self (McAdams, 1993). Many of the reflections are snippets about individual lives, struggles, experiences, and incidents that are important to them.

The intention in using narrative analysis is to better understand experiences of students of color. Of course, because narrative analysis is an interpretive discourse (Lyotard, 1984) the interpretation is open to different interpretations. This research is an inquiry into how meaning is given to experience, especially in narratives of personal experience about concrete life situations of the history they studied.

In all three years, students reflected about the struggles they had with the novel, but they also found positive attributes amongst the challenges experienced:

> The idea that motivated me the most was actually the topic that I could find no rhyme, reason, or enjoyment from. This topic was the assignment of reading the book entitled *Baudolino* . . . but after reading *Baudolino*, I believe I was able to fully understand the point of not being biased. I do not think I would have been able to understand this clearly without class discussion (male, year two).

Students wrote often concerning valuing the social act of discussing their reading in groups and respecting the insights of other students even if they disagreed with them. This was mentioned multiple times as key to getting a deeper understanding of world history as a discipline, "I have learned that hearing the views on a topic from my classmates helps me clarify my own view" (male, year one).

In all three years students wrote enthusiastically concerning the social act of discussing the books:

> One of the activities from class that I feel helped me the most were the classroom discussions we had over both our readings and the lecture material we covered in class. These discussions would oftentimes force me to reach my own conclusions quickly, while being able to expound upon them to my peers and the instructors (male, year one).

Students also concentrated on the necessity of obeying the basic rules of the discipline, such as the need for multiple reliable sources, and this was coupled with a wariness of "Green Honey," a hallucinogenic drug used by Baudolino and friends to induce fantastic flights of fancy:

> The readings of *Baudolino* and Marks's book were most helpful because I learned many things from the discussions and analysis of the readings themselves. The first thing I learned from these readings was that it is very important to verify sources. Whether a history is made up of fairy tales or a fairly historical narrative with a hint of bias, it is crucial for teachers to evaluate the sources they use as supplemental materials for lessons before incorporating them into the class . . . it is necessary to compare them with other viable sources and read through them in order to discern bias or "green honey" from the facts (female, year two).

The real fear of "fake news" is an issue that plagues present-day society. Helping students to recognize and sift through fantasies was viewed by the students as "helpful" in reframing and validating how they would teach history. Had students been given a "reliable history" to read, it is argued the fault lines running through it frequently are not as easily spotted as they are in *Baudolino*.

Religion and Identity

Reading *Baudolino* repeatedly encouraged students to reflect deeply on issues of religious differences and identity. The United States prides itself on religious liberty and the separation of church and state, but this is increasingly juxtaposed especially in the "Bible Belt" of the southern states with the political power of evangelic Christianity. This student's focus is on religious differences but the connection between the absurdity of race and racism is flagged when he acknowledges "damaging tendencies":

> After arriving at Pndapetzim, Baudolino meets a skiapod and blemmyae. Skiapods and blemmyaes have different understandings of Christianity and they both perceive their own denomination as the accurate version. . . . Baudolino teaches that a debate on the accuracy of a religion is arbitrary. Furthermore, he teaches the perspectives approach by breaking down the damaging tendencies of "us and them" (male, year one).

Students wrote that *Baudolino* gave them a better understanding of how history is made and the perils inherent in relying on a single historical storyline:

> I think the dangers of presenting or knowing only one story is the most important over-arching theme of our course. From *Baudolino*, we considered how history is laced with myths, warped/differing perspectives, and inaccuracies (female, year two).

It is recognized that students using the same words may have different meanings attached. However, from exploring their choice of words and sentence structures, they have striking similarities and suggest students made comparable interpretations of their readings but they are open to interpretation (Boje, 2008):

> More than anything, my time in this course has taught me the importance of perspective in world history. Beginning with *Baudolino* I came to understand that the personal experience of a historian or story teller can have a strong impact on the story they tell. Personal bias, imagined details, hyperbole, and past

experiences all shape the story being told. . . . By approaching history from a different perspective, I learned that there are no simple causes to global events, and to do so from assumed knowledge leads to ignorance and misattribution of both cause and effect in world history (male, year two).

Baudolino often made students more aware that history is made, and personal and national biases may influence the choice of what history is taught both in terms of content and teaching methodology. They recognized that as educators they might invalidate multicultural groups because they knowingly or unknowingly reframe their experiences through a personal worldview.

Issues of culture, identity and religious affiliation are probably now more than ever educational undercurrents in the United States, (Omni and Winant, 1991), and these challenges are dealt with in a non-threatening manner in *Baudolino*. The tendency to see race in terms of color and to automatically conclude that "different" means "wrong," is acknowledged by students in the way Eco deals with such issues. In one instance there is an encounter with mythical creatures who cannot tell that they are different from each other.

When Baudolino's group attempts to explain the difference between Gavagai, who is a skiapod—a creature from White mythology that has one gigantic leg—and a blemmyae—another mythological creature with eyes, nose, and other facial features fixed within its torso—Gavagai fails to understand their peculiar logic. This can be an uncomfortable conversation for some students who are used to thinking in dichotomies, as it leaves them to query why arbitrary categories like race, that are often dependent upon observations of relatively slight physiological differences, figure so significantly in the history of the past and the present.

The inability to talk about race in many American classrooms without raising hackles is overcome with comedy as it often is in standup routines. The complexities of race and issues surrounding it are frequently underscored. Indeed, this apparently farcical conversation in *Baudolino* for students assumes the basis for a thoughtful discussion about a topic causing discomfort in many classroom contexts. When analyzing this encounter students commonly said they were more aware of their own culture and blind spots. Reading this text also demonstrates that cultures often have expectations about the "proper" way to write history, that their "logical" way of authoring history is not the same the world over, and that people from cultures whose "logical" way of writing history is circuitous, may do so in a style that to the White American eye lacks organization and is underdeveloped (Lustig and Koester, 2013).

If educators are frequently more attuned to this, they will be more likely to give such students appropriate and effective tools to thrive in teaching and being taught in an American history classroom, teaching students the White American critical need to think in broad historical contexts, question their sources, weigh their evidence and draw their own conclusions and the problems that arise if they do not. *Baudolino* portrays foundational aspects of learning history in an amusing and thought-provoking manner that draws the reader in and creates a multidimensional learning tool.

Origins

The Origins of the Modern World, a slim volume of just over 245 pages, is a "global and ecological narrative from the fifteenth to the twenty-first century," and unlike *Baudolino*, it is succinct. First it debunks the Eurocentric notion of European exceptionalism being the cause for the rise of the West, then suggests that historical contingency, accident, and conjuncture are perhaps more realistic explanations. Starting with China, the author weaves a compelling alternative narrative. Students find debunking the exploits of Baudolino rather easy because he is after all a lying historian. Evaluating a well put together argument by a traditional historian is another matter.

Eurocentric "Exceptionalism"

Using *The Origins of the Modern World* students are asked to read with a critical eye. They are asked to examine the way Marks puts his argument together, look for key concepts and different viewpoints and evaluate the arguments as they read. Many students are probably unaware or choose to ignore the way one's beliefs and worldview influence how they see history. This book uses a non-Eurocentric approach, and this comes as a surprise to many of the students who have not experienced such an un-Eurocentric continuous storyline. They have all taken most of the required content for their degrees, but this is for most the first time they have encountered an alternative history concerning the rise of the West as required reading, and some are resistant and defensive, others not:

> Instead of regarding the significant progress that the west makes, Marks often attempts to point out the environmental consequences of the industrial revolution, rather than the great benefit it had on the history of humanity. Unfortunately, Marks does not address the most significant factors in the rise of the West. Those factors include western philosophy, such as Greek and Roman philosophy (male, year three).

Marks discussed the rise of the modern world from a non-Eurocentric point of view, which was new to me. Not only is it important for one to think critically and attempt to view different perspectives, it is important to attempt to get students to do so as well (male, year one).

This is reminiscent of research by Wertsch (1994) mentioned in chapter 2, who wrote that the way students had been socialized and taught impacted on their ability to function with alternative historical narratives. The reflections of the students imply that what Wertsch and others found is to some extent still true of these students:

The Origins of the Modern World demonstrated how to provide the detail and reasoning that I will hope to bring to my students so that they can more fully understand events throughout history beyond the fact that they just happened. It became clear early on in class that it is important as a future teacher, and historian, to always consider who the presenter of the information is. That you could get a completely different account of a historical event depending on who is telling it; essentially, there is almost always more than one story (female, year three).

It is acknowledged and appreciated that reading a text which seems to go against cherished beliefs may create a certain amount of disbelief and anxiety, and one topic which did this was the way Marks dealt with the attacks on the United States in 2001.

Alternative Narratives

In the introduction to his book Marks writes that one of the purposes of his book is to explain September 11 in the context of a much wider historical tradition. Only one student in the three years mentioned this argument directly:

The targets of the World Trade Center and the Pentagon reveal where Al Qaeda's resentment lays, not necessarily western society. If Al Qaeda's goal was creating a clash of cultures, then targeting the Acropolis, Vatican, or Louvre would have been equally effective targets. The rise of the western world, at the expense of the rest of the world has bred resentment in areas such as Afghanistan where people have been repeatedly suffering under the hands of western ideal-driven nation-states who believe their particular form of ideology will "fix" the country (male, year two).

The fact that only one student made a direct reference to this argument may speak volumes. For students taking this class, holding, let alone expressing such views probably seemed unpatriotic. The silence of the students on this argument is deafening and suggests that even if they agreed with the discrediting of European exceptionalism as being a reason for the rise of the West, they are often unwilling to consider, or perhaps voice agreement in the classroom for an alternative narrative for this event. The other student mentioned 9/11 in reflections critiquing presentations:

> Many recent historical events could have been linked to this lesson plan such as the Palestinian Apartheid, or the attacks on 9/11. I would have related the topic to students if it had been my lesson plan. Furthermore, I would have made the students break into groups to talk about different perspectives of each major religion and draw their own conclusions about current events and determine for themselves what role religion plays in history today (female, year one).

Again these views were exceptions; on this topic students were not willing to take the risk.

Prior to the United States presidential election of 2016, and the election of populist leaders around the world, in places such as Brazil and India, one of the goals of school history was to promote cohesiveness in communities. This would be furthered by helping students understand their own cultural roots and the similarities they have with the rest of the world. The rise of populist politics has increased the focus on differences, renaming them exceptionalism. This student maintains attitude and way of teaching is not helpful for multicultural students:

> The subject of world history in the high school I attended was more of an extension of American history. As a minority student born in another country, I could not identify myself in the learning and I never really got to see different perspectives other than our "western ideology." I understand the importance of promoting national pride and national identity, but I feel like understanding the world and the different points of view makes us better citizens (male, year two)."

School history was once seen as one of the main vehicles for fostering the idea of global connections and the interdependence of people. Regrettably, some studies have suggested rather than creating cohesiveness, aspects of history and the way it is taught can frequently alienate students, especially multicultural students (Levstik, 2000). The significance of engaging students in "marginalized" histories may be diminishing as countries put themselves "first."

Unfortunately, fostering the abilities of middle and high school students to focus on such issues plus think in a broad historical context, question their sources, weigh their evidence and draw their own conclusions is now more than ever needed but not always uppermost in American school history classrooms. History teachers labor to "cover" the content curricula of state programs while also teaching students to find information, problem solve, and think critically.

This weighty task, coupled with struggling with the ever increasing demands of standardized testing may leave many (to the detriment of the discipline) involved in school history education with little room to concentrate on the critical skills of disciplined inquiry.

Eras

In year three students were introduced to a new text alongside Marks's *The Origins of the Modern World*. Burke, Christian, and Dunn's *World History for Us All: The Big Eras: A Compact History of Humankind for Teachers and Students* (*Eras*) gives readers a wide-angled lens to view the world. The view is linear and encompasses a history of the universe. It emphasizes how much the world has in common. The book begins with a variety of creation stories from around the world and slowly explains the beginnings of the universe, the Earth and human life in scientific terms.

Students are again challenged to fault the argument in a well-written book, and in reading this textbook are encouraged to note where these may lie. The White American culture of querying sources, asking questions and challenging evidence to lead to answers is evident in *Eras* as much as it is implied in *Baudolino*. Students work out that this way of thinking is cultural and that they may well teach students that think it is rude to ask questions and wrong to question their teachers. In the US the saying "the squeaky wheel gets the attention or grease" (depending on what side of the Atlantic you are on) and the Japanese proverb of "the stake that sticks up gets hammered down," deftly illustrate this issue (Lustig and Koester, 2013).

Eras is set out in an easy to read formula and inviting graphics give life to seeing world history as history for everyone. The book and the accompanying PowerPoints are perhaps useful tools that answer some basic questions teachers have when looking at world history, such as "where do you start?" and "how can you possibly teach it all?" In the not so distant past to teach world history in American or British schools was generally easy to plan and teach. Students were given a knowledge of Western Europe and other places got a brief mention usually from a "when WE got there" perspective.

Times have changed, and a variety of imperatives make this approach unacceptable. In American schools the changing demography of the country is one such imperative, as are technological, economic and global changes. Teaching history is for many a discipline that situates, gives structure and coherence and a sense of who they are or may become. The idea of discovering different perspectives, and cultures is suggestive of students learning to value diversity:

> When I'm teaching a lesson, I may only have one side of the story I am teaching. A student in my class may have another side of the story and I need to be open to the fact that it can be completely different from my story (female, year two).

Reading the texts created an awareness in students of "the big picture" and deeper understanding of how this picture could influence their teaching and students. It was, and it was not, surprising to learn that students had never encountered, or perhaps recognized alternative narratives, or the concept of Eurocentrism, and the notion that history is not static. This was the United States where at times the past and present collide and obscure in equal measure.

Eurocentrism

The Origins of the Modern World

Cohorts of students often voiced similar opinions, suggesting, as some said in their reflections, that discussions helped them clarify their opinions. In year one several students wrote they had never heard the terms "Eurocentric" or "European exceptionalism" or if they had heard the term they never realized just how much of the narrative was accepted without question.

In years two and three, students wrote concerning new ideas gained from *The Origins of the Modern World*. Unlike cohorts in year one they did not indicate the newness of the concept "Eurocentric." Throughout, comments on *Origins* were often in conjunction with reflections about *Baudolino*, which was unsurprising as they read the books in quick succession, and the books had been aligned in the course to enable students to make comparisons:

> The whole concept of Eurocentrism was a new concept to me, as I'd never realized how much I'd learned about world history was very much deeply rooted in Europe, and everything else was either merely skimmed over or left out entirely.... The readings and class discussions also got me thinking outside of the

box: *Baudolino* and the idea of embellishing history, or Marks (de)constructing a Eurocentric view on why the modern world is the way it is (male, year one).

Additionally students who commented on the Eurocentric nature of history were aware of it to some extent, but did not have the tools of an alternative narrative to counter the argument:

> I have always felt that history was a culmination of contingency, and conjecture, but could never put it into words. *Origins of the Modern World* clarified history for me. It also brought to my attention how Eurocentric history can be. I have always advocated teaching from multiple viewpoints, but I never realized how ingrained the Eurocentric view is in the field of history and in modern American Society. I now know to be more careful about the information I present as fact (female, year one).

Students thought Marks's argument about "the Gap" was helpful in giving them ideas of how to give students they would teach an explanation for why there are haves and have-nots in the world:

> I feel that the explanation of the gap is the best way to understand how the world society has become. I will use this information to give the students a better understanding because they need to understand that things will continue this way if nothing is changed (female, year three).

Differences in Students' Data

Eras

In Year three *Big Eras* was introduced as a class text. The comments included the helpfulness of the book in terms of giving an overview of the world's history in a succinct manner that could be adapted to any state's standards.

One factor evident from the analysis of students' reflections over the three years was the nature of critiques. In year three, self-identified non-White American students as in other years were more likely to focus on issues of identity, mispronunciation of culturally linked words by fellow students, and flaws in knowledge about minorities. White American students reflected in general terms on issues such as their reading. For example, the following two students spoke from the same year:

> The Big Eras book helped me to have a timeline of the major periods of history. It helped me gain a better understanding of the chronological order of events

which will help me to be a better teacher when making a lesson plan for a certain era (female, year three).

There are many ethnicities within the United States and the numbers for each are constantly on the rise. Although there are differences amongst generations there are some who will always be viewed based on their appearance, regardless if they are a fourth generation immigrant who shares no ties with the nation their great-grandparents came from. Therefore, the matter of identity is a major factor that needs to be addressed (female, year three).

Overall it is significant that students wrote concerning the transferability and critical pragmatism of the course as is indicated by the following examples:

Much of what we learned can be put to use in other ways like at work or in another class or just when discussing things with friends (female, year two)

We were taught a variety of ways to coax this participation such as activities, uncomfortable silence, questioning, and even getting angry. Each of these tactics was used during class to facilitate participation many times without the class even realizing this was what was happening (male, year one).

Conclusion

The reflections do indicate that students report a change in ideas and a greater understanding of the discipline they may be preparing to teach. The reflections also strongly suggest that issues of identity are probably uppermost in the minds of multicultural participants. The data did reveal that self-identifying students of color were more likely to link issues of identity with themselves and White students' remarks were much more general. This is reminiscent of research detailed in previous chapters of this book concerning students of color, who were much more concerned with issues of identity in their history lessons than White students.

In a time when getting social-media "selfie" students to engage with textbooks is becoming increasingly rare, and perhaps old-fashioned, the fact that students were engrossed and uncovered content and formulated new meanings and ideas is significant for teacher education. Students will if required often read long books and alternative narratives. Moreover, they valued and respected the act of discussion and connected it to understanding the rules of their discipline more thoroughly. Furthermore, in lesson presentations students did try to put into practice what they had learned during their reading and discussions:

X Y, Z, and I presented our lesson on Islam's origins, early expansion, the Sunni and Shia split, and Baghdad in the year 1000. The lesson commenced with a hook activity to enable students to learn about Islam without prejudices and bias. Students were instructed to express their thoughts or first impressions about Islam on post-it notes and put them on the doorway. After the students posted their thoughts on the doorway, they walked through the door, thus symbolizing the refreshing of the minds. Subsequently, this activity opened their minds for the subject matter within the lesson (female, year two).

A critical sign of mastery in learning is transfer and this data hints that approaching the teaching of world history through literature is a small step toward seeing and teaching the world in more inclusive ways. As the researcher writes, sitting on a bookshelf is a tiny jar found on a lectern where they had been invited as a guest speaker some months after teaching one of these classes. On the jar is a homemade label saying "Green Honey" a reminder of the hallucinating potion in *Baudolino*.

CHAPTER EIGHT

Cultivating Curiosity, Complexity and Authentic Engagement in History Classrooms for Students of Color

This chapter is devoted to culturally responsive pedagogical issues and content that will probably more readily engage students of color as they learn history. It is interspersed with guiding questions and comments from students' interviews and reflections.

Prerequisites and Preparations

The following four prerequisites are frequently critical in facilitating intrinsic motivation among students of color at any educational level:

- Establishing a stimulating yet comfortable culturally responsive classroom climate
- Negotiating course expectations and behaviors
- Developing new competencies by building on prior knowledge and successfully completed tasks
- Giving students enough instruction to guide without undermining self-perceptions of control in both student and teacher.
- Creating authentic rigorous and relevant assessments

  1. Establishing a stimulating yet comfortable culturally responsive classroom climate

When students walk into classrooms, what tells them they are welcome?

This is not superficial—classroom climate also concerns seemingly surface issues as to whether all students feel welcomed. Reflect on how power and privilege impacts on what is taught in history and how this impacts students, school and communities. Perceptions dominate how you see the world and first impressions linger (Fraser, 1986). Whose face do you look for first in a group photograph, or a list of names where you know you should be included?

> I think that it is essential for Black children to know their history. Not just pictures on the wall. Because it is not taught as much as White history in most schools and Black children are not told the roles that Black people played in history, so they do not think they have achieved anything (Ebbe, 16).

In order to foster enhanced learning climates that nurture students of color and create complexity, diversity and connectedness, educators must examine the following:

- If the learning climate is often one of "fear," how do you limit the ultimate fear, the fear of failure?
- Is learning a process or a product?
- Do you see students of color as having the ability to think and act on their own during history lessons?
- Do you tolerate or enable educational apathy, detachment, and failure in students of color?
- Do you recognize White power and middle-class privilege at play in your classrooms and society?
- How do you make history lessons exciting and thought provoking for students of color?
- How do you become more democratic in the classroom?

Many educators struggle to better serve students whose cultures are different from their own. This cultural mismatch is a known factor in students' academic performance and the achievement gaps among students of color. The fundamentals of effective history instruction to students of color are frequently the attitudes and expectations of educators coupled with communication, diverse history content, and versatile teaching strategies.

Attitudes and Expectations of Educators

Foremost, it is advisable to self-examine and face personal prejudices, attitudes and the beliefs both educators and students hold. Educators need consistent awareness of how experiences and worldview shape and mold various roles they play in life. There should be deeper understanding of how knowledge, beliefs and skills interact with students' value systems and comprehension during instruction. Furthermore, it is essential to evaluate the extent to which educators accept different cultures, customs, traditions and values. Consider the ways you may be contributing to inequity by tolerating educational apathy.

What do teachers know about the systems that oppress people of color? Are educators' classroom practices habitually reinforcing plantation-like structures of silence around students of color? Considering these aspects, how can educators actively honor the differences they meet in the classroom and the wider community (Hollins and Govan 2015)?

Communicating

Research points out that history lessons can be traumatic and oppressive for students of color. They can feel silenced. They question their self-worth because of the omissions of their histories and cultures in history classrooms and daily life. Moreover, they are recurrently victims of identity abuse suffered at the hands of educators and peers. This kind of trauma will almost undoubtedly lead to withdrawal or apathy toward the subject.

In order to be more successful at history, all students need to practice answering questions and discussing new material if they are to begin to build on prior knowledge and master the new knowledge. If the new knowledge they are receiving habitually traumatizes and collides with lived experiences, they will probably not receive satisfaction from completing their work (Hollins and Govan, 2015).

It is well documented that students of color get less attention from teachers, are called on less frequently, and are asked fewer and lower-order questions. They are rarely asked to explain how they reached a given conclusion. They are seldom asked to reflect critically about issues. Moreover, the questions these students pose concerning the history they study along with comments they make, are more likely to be ignored. It is not surprising then to find students of color are silent and silenced in history classrooms.

Students of color are also less likely than their White counterparts to receive praise and are criticized more frequently. If praised, the acclaim tends to be terse and formulaic. Feedback is often more generic than appropriately detailed. And compounding this there is discipline disproportionality.

Considering this, effective educators will need to ask their students of color more and higher-order questions and provide multiple assignments that promote critical and higher-order thinking. Teachers should praise more and criticize less. They need to return personalized and instructive feedback on assignments verbally or in written form. And they should aim to check for understanding by asking students to explain how they reached a conclusion or get them to defend a taken position.

Effective teachers of students of color are usually those determined and careful to assess history narratives concerning diverse students. They continually recognize the differences between equity, equality, and systems of oppression and try hard to act accordingly. They see, or at the very least try to see how privilege and access to opportunities affect educational success, identifying the deficit model and how it connects to the academic achievement gap. Moreover, they have plans of action to thwart this that lead to changes in their own practice.

Building Relationships

Accepting and respecting students of color, and applying knowledge concerning their cultures, when planning and implementing instruction are recurrently prerequisites of trust building. Using knowledge about the lives of students to inform teaching practices and to establish trust with students is repeatedly strategically crucial. It is also necessary to take into consideration power relationships in schools and classrooms and aim to act on the way we communicate verbally and nonverbally with students of color during history lessons.

Time is needed to develop productive, effective relationships with students of color, and this will in turn frequently improve classroom management. It will probably also help develop student motivation and engagement in the history classroom. But underlining this is the continuing need for educators to advance personal and interpersonal skills by self-monitoring interactions with these students. Cultivating awareness and sensitivity to classroom dynamics is key, as is understanding personal attachment and identifying with a culture that may vary among students. One size will frequently not fit all.

Taking into consideration how students of color may see you as the teacher is one of the main pillars of building understanding and trust. Plan for this. Trust will not always be instantaneous, and students may often doubt your sincerity. Observe and listen, ask for their perspectives, and incorporate these into teaching. Students of color have lived experiences that jar with the dominant narratives found in social studies texts. The advent of "fake news" has for many led to a breakdown of trust in the press and figures of "authority."

History instruction with good historical reasoning has always to some extent been problematic for students of color with regard to trust. Helping students to understand the importance of verifying with reliability of sources, not just ones that support their opinions, has constantly been in the remit of history teachers. However, students should be taught the right to disagree, as well as the right to change their minds about an issue based on the available evidence.

The history classroom should be safe, supportive and equitable. This should be the constant norm. Again, communication and building relationships so that students feel comfortable working on sensitive topics without fear of censor from their peers or the silent condemnation of teachers is crucial. The silencing of voices by educators through "silence" is probably even more damaging than that of classmates. Look for the triggers, the micro aggressions in the history classroom that are often subtle, are usually unintended and may sound "funny" to some but are hurtful and alienating to the student at which they are directed. We need to shift below the remarks as well as not tolerate the behavior, no matter how innocuous it may sound. At the first infraction we should act.

Linguistically Relevant and Responsive Pedagogy
One neglected aspect is to explore the linguistic backgrounds of culturally diverse students of color. Language barriers are always present in some form in the classroom. The author's United Kingdom English and British idioms at times unknowingly mask meaning for American students. How much more so when English is an additional language. Having students read a passage in its original language and then reading it in English is one way of doing this. Whether that language is Spanish, or an English or French Patois, it will probably give students who identify with heritages that speak such languages a sense of belonging and ownership of what they are studying (Showstack, 2012). The pronunciation of words and content are frequently important, as this student writes:

> He had a very "whatever" approach when it came to certain content and the pronunciation of foreign words. As a minority, I can become very disinterested in a class where the professor stereotypes mine or other cultures and does not give it respect by lack of effort. There is a lot of diversity in classrooms and so it would have been better for him to use his foreign students' help with the pronunciation and such. They need to try to think about what kinds of questions the students will most likely ask them as well (Lizette, 22).

Paying attention to academic language and strategies to help students of color acquire and use spoken academic language to enhance the development of written history assignments will often also help teachers meet accountability and quality assurance requirements.

Families and Communities
Effective teachers recognize the value of families and communities of color in educational success. Educators need to move from a default position of thinking that low income, education and a person's cultural background impact negatively on the way they perceive education. All parents are frequently involved in some manner in the education of their children (Henderson and Mapp, 2002).

Proactively demonstrating real interest in students' lives both inside and outside of the classroom pays dividends. One should not be interfering; therefore, set boundaries with which everyone is comfortable. What do educators know and need to know about students in terms of their cultural identities and backgrounds? Well, as much, or as little, as they choose to disclose. Some students will frequently be forthcoming and others may think it is none of their business, and educators should not assume that just because they have people who look as if they are part of a cultural group that they actually are.

There is great need to develop cultural knowledge of different groups and with practice master teaching across cultures. Furthermore, more attention should be given to the possible way school-home connections of students of color affect personal unofficial histories. Perhaps contemplate how this may impact the way school history and dominant narratives are frequently interpreted and sometimes discarded. Students of color need to feel and think that teachers see them as whole people who are often respected in terms of their intellect and the assets they have to offer. Therefore, valuing and respecting historical and lived experiences are foundational.

Effective teachers build bridges from the prior knowledge of students to new information, in much the same way as historians build incomplete bridges to the past. Teaching history means undoubtedly teaching controversial issues and having a duty of care to ensure classroom climate is accepting, comfortable, and collaborative for all students. As this student reminds, there is the need of sensitivity when instructing young minds:

> Well, maybe you should talk to the teacher, making sure that the teacher [pause] says, "yeah this is how it was, but don't let this put you off." "Cos really this was still children they are teaching it to. As long as they are explaining it well, then there is no reason why that shouldn't be shown. It's the truth (Shannon, 17).

Activity—Classroom Climate

The first day of class involves an icebreaker that allows the students to interact and find out some of their surface quirky similarities:

> Students are given four simple scenarios that will entail making choices, placing them into four different groups in the four corners of the room. For example, if you were an animal what would you be—lion, tiger, elephant, giraffe? Or "you have been invited to a wedding and your choices of main course are beef, chicken, fish, vegan." Which would you choose? Once in their group they introduce themselves to each other. Then give them another scenario and once again they probably move to another group. This activity leads to a lot of laughter and students find out more about their neighbors than their names. It takes a very short time and the rewards are often huge. They are frequently doing something unexpected, and in a non-threatening approach they reveal aspects of themselves to each other and the teacher. Even if only trivial things, they realize what they have in common. This gives the opportunity to gain a sense of community in a short period of time.

Consistently demonstrate attitudes that honor and value the diversity of your students, and histories, cultures, and languages that they may see as their own. Find multiple ways to infuse them into your teaching.

2. Negotiating expectations and behaviors

Set and maintain high expectations consistently for learners and yourself. Establishing what is expected of the students in terms of the core objectives of the assignment or course is essential. Students need to believe they can satisfy all the requirements of a given assignment or course of study. Therefore, there is the strong need for applying an asset model to characterize students of color. The perceived inferiority of cultures of students of color and stereotypes are often so instilled in some classrooms that many of these students may reject their culture and live up to their teachers' low expectations rather than their parents' aspirations (Patel, 1994, pp. 9–14).

Of course, stereotypes are mental shortcuts. If every time one saw a chair one had to work out what it was, one would take an inordinate amount of time working out what the "chair" was in all its various forms. However, structural racism used in stereotypes to justify a framework of derogatory beliefs concerning people of color has become almost "commonsensical" notions. The historical idea of people of color being inferior, and the bottom in a hierarchy of races, has bled from the past into the present and undoubtedly will seep into the future.

Expect, require and facilitate the engagement of all students in both thinking and learning during history lessons. Educators should make sure praise and affirmation in the classroom are evenly spread and that they are sincere. All students recognize fake praise as easily as they can spot a preservice teacher. Once educators know the likes and dislikes of their students, they can include or avoid these as much as possible in their instruction.

Mentor your students of color. You are not their friend, but you should be their supporter. Consistently redirect unengaged students when instructing and use motivational strategies to stimulate all students. School for some students of color is akin to the boxing ring, and they need to know there is someone in their corner with balm and pep talk urging them on to learn from their mistakes and giving them the confidence to "fight" another round.

Use consistent and convincing evidence of scaffolding for all students while maintaining a high level of cognitive demand and require higher order thinking from all students. Provide opportunities for all students to work within their zone of proximal development. Teachers should give students of color opportunities to think creatively and independently, and frequently provide students with limited English proficiency choices in how they demonstrate history content knowledge.

Activity—Negotiating Expectations and Behaviors
Ask students to say what they enjoy and dislike about history classes. Give them ten minutes individually generating lists of the best and the worst aspects of history classes. Then in groups of four or five have them share their lists. Next, have them compile a list of three things they hate, and three that they like or would like to see in their history lessons. The lists are always similar, and it is not onerous to come up with four to six things that they then turn into a list of seven ground rules for a history class. This is where the professor promises to try not to do those things and where students work out what they need to do if they are to get the most out of the semester.

By the end of the activity students begin to better understand that the most productive and engaging forms of learning occur when they are often actively engaged. The professor's hidden mantra of "just telling is not teaching and just hearing is not learning" is experienced by the students. The byproduct of this activity is students realize that their opinions are frequently valued by their peers and professor.

3. Developing new competencies by building on prior knowledge and successfully completed tasks.

Unspoken objectives of teachers and questions of students

The explicit and implicit objectives of any history course or assignment or unit are that the students commensurate to their ages will be able to

1. Demonstrate an effective command of a historical record
2. Write in a clear expository manner
3. Orally articulate and defend a clear and concise argument
4. Analyze historical evidence

Four unspoken questions are uppermost in students' minds whenever they approach an assignment, topic or take a class:

1. *Is this interesting?* The need for novelty and curiosity (Montgomery, 1954).
2. *Am I able to do this?* The need for perceptions of competence and control (Bandura, 1985).
3. *What do I have to do to be successful?* The need for a directing component (Anderson & Jennings, 1980).
4. *What will I gain if I do it?* (The desire for rewards or the fear of punishments (Entwistle, 1987).

Research contends that perceptions of competence and control are recurrently prerequisites for the highest levels of competence. Perceived competence seems to be more important than perceived control in explaining an individual's task-related engagement. If a person perceives herself as highly competent in a given situation, then opportunities to take control of that situation will be frequently meaningful to her and likely to lead to an increased level of task-related engagement.

That said, if a person does not perceive herself as very competent, then opportunities to take control of the situation will often be meaningless at best and threatening at worst. Hence, without some level of perceived competence, some individuals will probably never perceive themselves as having any real control over a situation (Good & Brophy, 2007).

Key unspoken implicit objectives educators should apply concerning students of color (SOE) are outlined in the chart below:

122 ～ Chapter Eight

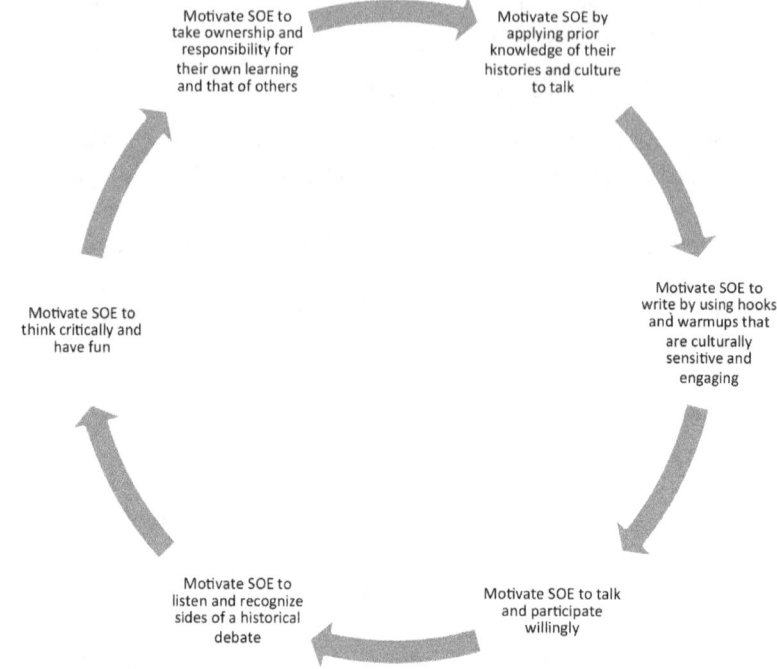

Unspoken implicit objectives

A most important task of any history class is persuading students to explore histories in ways that will commonly spark their curiosity and at the same time cultivate complexity. To be effective educators must use relevant literature, their own experiences and information and communication technology (ICT) to enhance history lessons for students of color.

Reading and Writing

Experience and common sense teach that even the most diligent of students sometimes fail to see the value of assigned readings when they are frequently not expected to utilize what they have read in a meaningful way. If readings become irrelevant background noise and fail to connect with the content of the lecture or presentation or activities, then students may not appreciate the relevance unless the magical words "there may be a surprise quiz on this" are uttered. This is a pity, as research shows that probably the best form of motivation is intrinsic interest mixed with extrinsic rewards (Deci & Ryan, 2000).

In the author's experience the following strategy makes for rewarding results in terms of students' interactions with the assigned text and their class participation for older students.

Activity—Developing New Competencies

The technique used is straightforward as understandings of what makes for an effective and engaging class have been dealt with.

> Students agree that before each class they will write four sentences about their assigned reading. They can turn this in online or on paper. The key is they are given a choice as to what they will write about, and the subject matter is not specific, but it is limited to the chapter/s which curtails and focuses students. Their sentences are then used as jumping off points for class discussions. At the start of each class, students have to locate someone in the room that has written about the same thing, and then discuss what they found, and report back. If they neglect their four sentences on the first day, they never do it again as they are held accountable to the whole class. This activity may be varied by asking them to find someone that has written about something different. Then the students report back and the teacher facilitates discussion on these topics, bringing in additional information as and when necessary.

For further accountability the "sentences" may be collected and commented on rather than graded. However, just holding them accountable each class to bring something worthwhile to the discussion is enough of a motivator to keep them reading, and it also taps into their prior knowledge and experiences and helps create a sense of ownership toward their learning.

The following students' reflections give a brief flavor of their counter-stories and thinking:

> Oftentimes, when I think about the contributions Blacks have made to American civilization I don't think of horse racing. I was fascinated to learn they took part in this sport in the early 1600s. . . . While the sport was controlled by White aristocrats, many southern owners trained their young male slaves to be jockeys for their horses. The northerners did the same but used free Black men as jockeys. Blacks soon became some of the most talented riders and trainers of horses, North and South (George, 26).
>
> Just like then, the KKK is still around for the same purpose and most are still not facing any consequences, and that alone tells you about America. Black people in America, even after slavery, never fell for the idea of them being free. Sure, they may have had more rights than before but those were all just for show. The rise of Jim Crow proves that. Back to the fear of being equal, once they found out that we couldn't legally be owned, they found ways to segregate us. They still managed to place fear into any Blacks that tried to vote for the Lincoln party by violence, threats of losing job or home and those who overcame all of that, their votes were still manipulated by stuffing ballot boxes, removing unwanted votes or reporting fraudulent totals. As a whole, that

makes me think about the 14th and 15th amendment and if we were actually viewed as citizens and would have a say in who runs this country (Bryan, 21).

4. Giving students enough instruction to guide without undermining self-perceptions of control in both student and teacher.

Central to the educational process is the interactions between students and teachers. In order to become more democratic in the classroom, using the constructivist view of knowledge helps students to construct and reconstruct historical knowledge. Instruction and classroom should reflect a visually supportive environment that includes the lived experiences of students of color, their histories, language and cultures. Great care should be taken to apply differentiated strategies and students' personal histories in both planning and instruction, but educators should not confuse aimless coverage with learning.

Help students to work out that different perspectives on a historical event or person may change minds or enable them to see aspects of the past in new or different lights. The aim of good history teaching is transfer. Students of color should be able to use what they are learning. Exploring problems of the past in this manner will often aid students of color to use the past to answer questions of the present. At the heart of the educational process is the interaction that occurs between educators and students and with their peers.

When educators reflect on the gaps concerning responsive pedagogy in state standards, curriculum and teaching materials, they are prompted to incorporate additional material or at the very least acknowledge the gaps along with the students, such as pointing out the absence of Native Americans in most history texts except as a backdrop to European Colonization, the Trail of Tears and shadowy miniscule mentions of the group "Indians of All Tribes' and their occupation of Alcatraz and offering to buy back New York for $24, and "The Trail of Broken Treaties' occupations during the era of Civil Rights in the twentieth century.

Strategies and Methods
Keeping students engaged can be energizing and daunting. To encourage different perspectives and allow visual entry points into a topic it is useful to have students watch short documentaries and parts of films. These are not used as a method of "killing time" but help cater to the learning preferences in classrooms. Critical thinking is also promoted by having students analyze the components of historical films and their texts and material culture.

Educators may take it for granted that texts and media are created entities and that films, books, visual images have messages and purposes that a surface examination does not always reveal. Many students of color may have a well-developed sense of skepticism. Therefore, having them work out what the purpose of a source is (a key skill for the discipline of history), is exactly what they are often good at. Working in self-assigned groups of three, older students will often be prompted to note that films and to a large extent textbooks generally tell single stories, that they often have a moral tone and suggest a progressive view of history. Have students examine textbook jackets, titles, and chapter headings and get them to work out that textbooks have implicit messages.

Some students quickly recognize and are able to verbalize that historical films in general tend to focus on individuals and often use a fixed perspective rather than a number of alternative views. Together, work out the central message of the text and the emotive qualities that filmmakers attach, such as musical scores, to their products to entice and hook and guide their audience (Marcus, Metzger, Paxton, & Stoddard, 2010).

The following prompts are useful starting points for this exercise:

- Who created the message?
- What creative techniques are used to attract attention?
- How might different people understand this message?
- What values, lifestyles and points of view are represented in, or omitted from, this message?
- Why is this message being promoted?

Perspectives
Early in the semester, the issue of perspective and helping students better understand how we understand the past from different vantage points is crucial. Take your students on a "class trip." Decide on a part of the school and approach the building or room or item from a variety of angles. Get your students to say or write what they 'see." From this activity it is soon clear that depending on where a person is standing their perspective will regularly be different, or they may focus on different things. Guide them into understanding that history is "made," and different people will often notice different aspects. Chimamanda Adichie's TED talk "The Danger of a Single Story" is an excellent way to get your students thinking, talking and writing about perspectives in history as this student of Mexican heritage comments:

The second video that illustrated the dilemma created by a one narrative view of the world was the young novelist, Chimamanda Ngozi Adichie. As her story became more complex I did not expect her experience in Mexico. I saw how easy it was to fall prey to constant bombardment of stereotypes when she spoke of seeing the Mexicans as people who went to work, enjoyed shopping and eating and not just poor, drug addicted illegal immigrants. Hearing that her professor thought of her characters as not authentically African showed even educated people can pass judgment ignorantly. I realized that a teacher should not go into a class assuming that all have had the same experiences (Carlos, age 22).

The poem "The Blind Men and the Elephant" by John Godfrey Saxe is a useful hook to get students thinking about perspectives and problem-based learning when exploring history concerning colonialism, class, race, or religion.

The single-story students of color from the African diaspora are often told their history begins with slavery. As noted in the early interviews, students wanted stories of a past that included more positive aspects of what they considered their histories. While some curricula include the rise of a variety of African Kingdoms and individuals like Mansa Musa, more needs to be done to help students of color make connections to themselves. Such as the development of a coherent, long-term narrative, the big picture of historical episodes so that they can see where they fit in.

Students of color have their own ideas, beliefs and understandings of what history is and what it should be. Every child of color should know the continents and countries of the global south. Start with the sheer size of Africa. Point out the way this is distorted in maps used. The diversity of the Indian subcontinent in terms of languages, and peoples is often truncated into the French, British and Gandhi. The history of Japan is sometimes shorthand for Commodore Perry and Pearl Harbor, and Korea to the Korean War. China's diversity in terms of people, geography and climate is frequently skimmed over in a single lesson. In middle and high school students need to develop a chronological framework for the copious periods and events state standards mandate they learn. Admittedly, the textbook approach of "this happened, then that" may lead to some of the disconnectedness seen in students of color regarding the past.

Digital Frameworks
Students actively doing history are greatly aided by the use of digital sources. Using the internet educators can help them reconstruct, narrate and create. There are abundant artefacts, printed sources, and visual images that can spark the historical imaginations of students of color. They are also able

to create their own oral histories and devise games and simulations, and of course use it for communicating their own narratives, telling their personal histories and seeing how they fit into the big picture. For older students, educators may find the use of podcasts useful to frontload information; however, for students where access to reliable technology is an issue, this may be problematic.

Use websites that allow the placing of different countries into interactive maps of other places such as Africa. All students need to learn the names of the countries that make up this continent and a brief history of the most multiple tribes, languages and cultures in each of its countries. The scramble for Africa is in many curricula, but colonization, decolonization and recent history should not be ignored. Students of the African diaspora need to know their history does not begin with slavery. Project based learning is a good place to start. From interviews this is illustrated by Fred who chose to study Ghana and Jamaica:

> Interviewer: Okay, can you give me an example of the history of somebody else and when you feel it is your history?
>
> Fred: But when I feel it is my history was when they told you to study two countries and get loads of facts about the countries. Yeah, like famous people from that country and basically just show it in a report, in a poster or in, oh, you could present it in any way you like.

This kind of activity should not be placed at the end of the year where students know educators put placeholder areas to kill time before "important topics." Make sure the project has different stages and attached learning outcomes. Be strategic in making the project challenging with goals and provide "rest areas" along the way when you as facilitator give meaningful feedback. Do, however, allow students to make some decisions—do not micromanage them. Allow the students a measure of creativity and choice as motivational tools. When using group work, help students understand how groups work best and monitor them to ensure equity in workloads. Or know-it-all Norris may end up dominating and silent Sandra may find herself frozen out (Weinstein et al., 2019).

Identities and Social Groups

i. How do historical narratives lead to "in" groups and "out" groups? How can we counter such stories?

One way of exploring identities and social groups is to use children's stories such as *The Bear that Wasn't*, by Frank Tashlin (2007) or Dr. Seuss's *The Sneetches* (1953). Or depending on the age of students, take excerpts or all of H. Milner's (1956) *Body Ritual among the Nacirema*. To explore how others are dehumanized and made exotic, link this to episodes in history where people have been labelled and treated accordingly. Point out the emotive nature of words and how they may create trauma. Help students actively build on prior knowledge by getting them to brainstorm why some words are triggers for feelings of hurt and anger (Tatum, 1997).

For example, have a discussion of the word "slave" and why there is some resistance about using the word "enslaved" in some quarters. Demonstrate with examples the long worldwide history of enslaved people and that it is not just a North American phenomenon. Foreground, recognize and demonstrate through your teaching that the history of Black people in the Americas does not begin with enslavement. Rather it was an interruption. Jamaica Kincaid's (1985) "Columbus in Chains" is a short story that helps start the conversation of the impact of colonialism through a child's eye. Paule Marshall's (1983) "To Da-duh, in Memoriam" uncovers the rich histories of generations clashing and loving, and is a useful starting point for uncovering lived histories and personal connections to other countries. Edwidge Danticat's (1995) *Krik? Krak!* short stories do likewise for stories of migrant histories.

Discuss why the Eugenic movement, Social Darwinism, and Manifest Destiny help one better understand how prejudice, discrimination and exclusion and a sense of mission and the rightness of a cause may lead to a variety of holocausts. Include the Great Dying, which devastated Native Nations in the early colonial period, but remember to include facts and figures demonstrating that descendants of these people remain and thrive. Have students discuss why the word "survivor" is used as a term for some and not others when studying historical holocausts.

ii. How do the choices people made in the past impact us today? How might the choices people make today impact us in the future?
iii. What tools can we use to reduce prejudice and discrimination today?

Using casualty figures, acknowledge that there is a tendency to have a more accurate count of the dead of dominant groups in the past, and the present, both in peace and wartimes. Discuss why some perspectives have been viewed as more important than others. Get students to work out which voices are silent in stories and why this may be so (Hooks, 1994). Help them understand that textbooks fail to explain just how messy and complex history is. Timelines help students visualize the complexity of history. Help students work out why this might be. A useful starting point might be the Bai JuYi's poem, "The Old Man with the Broken Arm." Use this to study about the draft in United States history during the Civil War and conscientious objectors such as Mohammed Ali during the Vietnam War.

Counterfactual and Complex Histories

Counterfactual histories are one way to help students think about accidents and conjecture in history. What if the bullet that killed Abraham Lincoln had only grazed his temple? Would Reconstruction have had a different outcome for people of color? What if the bullet that killed Martin Luther King Jr. had ricocheted and lodged into the wall? Would the Civil Rights movement for people of color been different? Educators need to enable students of color to make clear deep connections from the 13th and 14th amendments to the United States Constitution, linked to claims from Civil Rights leaders in the twentieth century.

Have students work on the complexity of politicians such as Lincoln's views on race: Martin Luther King Jr and Malcolm X and groups like the Student Nonviolent Coordinating Committee (SNCC) and their approaches to civil rights.

Black Consciousness and the Building and Protecting of America

The Atlanta Compromise and the work of Booker T. Washington and W.E.B. DuBois come under scrutiny in many texts. Include the work of Marcus Garvey and his contributions to debates about the role of Black people in society and the complex reactions of DuBois and others. Readings from works such as Colin Grant's (2008) *Negro with a Hat: The Rise and Fall of Marcus Garvey* make for nuanced and compelling secondary sources. Compare the role of West Indians building the Panama Canal and the Chinese building the American Railroad system and their involvement in world wars, which are frequently neglected topics in schools as well as the twentieth century roles of people of Mexican American heritage in the agricultural life of the United States such as Dolores Huerta and Caesar Chavez's fight to improve agricultural working conditions in the United States, and the wealth of Latino/a literature. Such resources are often hidden in plain sight in many history classroom student bodies.

For example, there is a culture of growing and eating rice in parts of North America. In the United States today, descendants of these rice-growing Africans are called "Gullahs/ Geechee" and still live along the South Carolina and Georgia coast. The Gullah live in small farming and fishing communities and have preserved a strong African cultural heritage, probably because of their geographical isolation and a strong community life.

The creole the Gullah speak is like Sierra Leone Krio and West Indian English patois. They "use African names, tell African folktales, make African style handicrafts such as baskets and carved walking sticks, and enjoy a rich cuisine based primarily on rice. "Rice occupied a place of cultural importance in much of West Africa and continued to be of cultural importance to the descendants of the enslaved people brought to North America" (Tuten, 2010, p. 50).

Key to making any topic or subject interesting is creating connections to aspects of students' lives. It is the story that lies at the heart of every topic that is taught that will usually draw or alienate your students. In the classroom educators need to make historical figures less remote. History resurrects dead people and events and breathes life into them. Telling vignettes using a variety of texts, including visual sources, about dusty corners of lives and events helps to link them to the present. Research has shown that students of color are often attracted to active and participatory teaching approaches such as role-play, drama, presentations, discussions, debates and making replicas.

Slavery

> iv. How do choices that individuals or groups made in the past impact the present?
> v. How might the choices people make today impact the future?

Some material, particularly concerning slavery, is likely to be sensitive to individuals and clash with customs of the community. Community outreach and asset-based community development and building trust is essential. No history curriculum, no matter how big or how inclusive, will probably begin to meet the needs of students of color unless teacher educators and practitioners become more aware of the complexity of dealing with cultural diversity in the classroom.

Contexts of misunderstanding are often created, hopefully not because educators set out to alienate, but because they are careless, unaware or do not understand the communities they teach in.

It seems quite obvious that the discipline of history habitually uses language infused with emotion. "Imperialism," "slavery," "civilized," or "Palestine" in place of "Israel," are words that trip lightly off the tongue and can immediately raise the hackles of some, while enthusing others; therefore, the continuing need to be mindful of language used, or the inferences made concerning topics, events and people.

Teaching the American Civil War to American students is a controversial topic for Americans regardless of color. Some will probably never accept that the war was primarily about slavery and see the issue of states rights as paramount, and others cannot see how you can make slavery almost a by-product of the whole affair. Educators must walk a tightrope and use a balance pole of skills and heightened awareness of the wire if they are to make it safely to the end of the wire.

Warn college students that it is alright to feel some discomfort, but not suffering during history classes and point out that this is often when growth and learning take place. Preconceived notions and misperceptions are often strengthened or resolved through examining evidence that supports or confronts beliefs. Treat all questions and answers with respect. Of course, you need to discard the really off-the-wall silly ones, but also be prepared to navigate in another direction when you see things slanting toward a point of view that may be offensive.

There will often be an ongoing need to effectively interrupt and redirect negative behavior—yours and that of students. When you find yourself thinking that certain students are living up to the expectations and prejudices of some sections of society, stop and recalibrate. Admittedly this is not a groundbreaking observation, but it is sometimes hard to do. And most educators are probably at some point reluctant to admit that they might just be leaning a little too much in one direction.

Research by the author has shown that specific individual teacher attitudes rather than teaching methods are cited as reasons for students of color feeling disconnected in history classes. There was a lack of trust that students of color gave to messages they received from their history teachers about people of color. This finding concurs with early work by Epstein (1997) mentioned in chapter 2, concerning the credence that African American students gave to information from formal education.

Furthermore, studies also suggest that students thought that teachers should not be afraid of tackling emotive issues in their history classrooms, as they experienced this in their lives and needed confirmation of such factors within history (Levstik, 2000). Ideas expressed by the respondents in interviews indicate that some students of color thought of negative attitudes of peers and teachers about minorities in history as personal abuse of their identities. For example, Lee recounted the following microaggressions:

We had to pretend to be slaves. Everyone was Black slaves. And some of the kids were like saying, "Oh, it's easy to pretend to act Black, just act stupid," and stuff like that. And in history [lessons] people would make jokes like, "you wouldn't see White people puking up over each other," like when they were on the ships and they threw up (Lee, 15).

The responses from students of color indicate that the resulting hurt, anger, bewilderment and feelings of temporary exclusion could impact adversely on their learning experience. There is great support in psychological literature for the salience of students' attitudes toward learning. These are deemed important because they provide insights into inter-related issues in educational psychology, including personality, self-esteem, motivation and the optimal conditions for learning (Wilson, 1985, p. 12).

Factors that may help surmount attitudinal obstacles encourage the greatest motivation, and the best learning conditions are likely to be vital matters for understanding and changing the way history is perceived and improving the way it is taught. Researchers have argued that lessons must present students with learning experiences which hold their attentions not only briefly, but also can command their loyalties and passions (Covington, 1992, p. 235). However, the key issue for multicultural students was that they thought teachers should do so sensitively. The evidence indicates that multicultural students assumed that teachers should realize the people that they were teaching were "still children." This is a central observation in this book.

Learning environments should be temperate enough, and curricula broad enough, for views and understandings to be aired and challenged, thereby making the learning experience less traumatic and more satisfying for all those involved.

Activities—Collaborative Instruction
Collaborative learning along with its more structured sister cooperative learning, both share a philosophical outlook that recognizes diversity amongst students needs not only to be recognized but also respected, and given a conducive learning environment. Given the right tools all students can achieve academic success (Sapon-Shevin, 2007). It is well documented that these learning techniques create a sense of ownership, community and promote the idea that learning is an active process (McGlynn, 2001; Haenen & Tuithof, 2008).

Posing a statement such as "Capital punishment should be abolished in all states," have students form a line with those who agree strongly at one end, to those that disagree strongly at the other. Then fold the line. The most diametrically opposed students will commonly find themselves facing each other. The middle of the line will regularly have greater consensus. Then have students explain to each other why they agree or disagree with the statement. At the end each student needs to explain what their "partner" had to say about the issue. This helps teach students to listen and to see that there are multiple viewpoints on issues, and each has some basic beliefs supporting the stance.

Facts and figures from sources concerning the historic disproportionality of more people of color being executed than White people for similar crimes can then be discussed. Key to the success of this is making sure that an equal amount of evidence is available for the students to reach reasoned decisions, and having a planned debriefing discussion.

Using Material Culture
Have students also talk about their emotions on seeing an object that an enslaved person might have possessed. Ask students to imagine what different people at different times might make of such items, such as during the Civil War (1860s), the Civil Rights Movement (1960s), and the present Black Lives Matter Movement (2019). This helps students understand the changing interpretations, significance and symbolism of items at different time periods. Students make hypotheses about what the contents tell them about enslaved people and their society and then compare it to items they might take if forced to flee from home.

At a surface level, this strategy is deceptively simple but in the study of history significant. Examining the material culture of the past, like other primary sources, enables learners to see a bigger picture of the past and more fully understand the value and pitfalls of sources. Moreover, it may make history more relevant to students' everyday lives once they are frequently able to make connections from the past to the present.

5. Creating authentic rigorous and relevant assessments

Educators recognize they must use appropriate inclusive measures of pre and post assessments tailored toward the students they teach and the standards they must meet. Much has been written about assessment and as educators they are recurrently praised or hung out to dry by their results. Unfortunately, the results that tend to count are quantitative rather than qualitative. Educators need to assess for understanding. Students need to be able to apply what they have learned to a new situation.

However, whether it is a process—formal, informal, authentic, performance based—or an improvement assessment, it should be founded on research-based strategies that maximize academic success for students of color. For example, adjust questions, scaffold, and differentiate assessments based on the characteristics of individual students. We need to remember that assessments are often like individual photographs in an album—they show students at a given time.

Set the bar high and pull your students up. As has been said repeatedly, nothing breeds success like success. For a student to have really tried hard only to meet repeated failure is devastating. Students need to experience a measure of real success frequently to spur them on. If a student is using great effort and only meeting failure, then as teachers we are probably failing them. Of course, some students may think they are working hard when they are not. Therefore, the need to teach study skills is paramount as these are seldom taught. Differentiating lessons to meet needs is not "dumbing down," but it is catering to the needs of all students.

Adapting instruction to meet the needs of students of color and redirecting and reenergizing individual students to think and learn, using multiple learning preferences makes sense, as is having points in lesson plans when you can change direction or strategies to redirect or reaffirm student behavior and attitudes as you teach.

Help your students of color to acquire a more comprehensive knowledge of the subject. Engage in formative and summative assessment of their work using culturally responsive and linguistically relevant pedagogy so as to understand where learning gaps frequently are and to improve instruction and learning outcomes. Use technology as an integral tool to assess learning in the classroom (Gay, 2010). Encourage your students to be accepting of themselves and others. History lessons should help develop an understanding of histories, traditions and perspectives of specific groups. Help your students to value diversity and equity. Equip all students with the tools to work actively toward a more equitable society.

Activity—Testing with Less Fear
Building off the previous activity of students choosing three or four topics from their reading is an activity that works well in large classes.

The instructor prepares by leaving around ten markers at the Whiteboard. At the start of the lesson the instructor asks students to write a word or phrase on the board concerning their topic. Coming to the front in groups of ten or so students, they write their words or phrases down. Once they are used to the exercise students as they enter the room will often automatically write their words on the board without prompting.

Use those words in a variety of ways. First read aloud what has been written. Then either have students talk about their word or have a volunteer come to the front and the rest of the class must make links between the topics or perhaps put them in chronological order. The volunteer on the direction of other students draws lines or circles from one word to another. Students enjoy this exercise and by varying what you do with the words students are habitually kept attentive and active. The instructor may also correct misunderstandings and elaborate on particular words. It makes for an informative and inclusive review of class readings.

In Summary
Teaching history courses to students of color in multiple grades, which is often viewed by some students as doing something they know already, may seem a thankless and even tedious task. Research, anecdotal and media based on the other hand, points fingers at the ignorance of the general public concerning American History (Wineburg, 2001). School teachers were once the main target of this "failure," but the finger is now being pointed at those who prepare teachers.

Among a long list, teacher preparation courses stand accused of producing skills without knowledge, of being remote from what goes on in schools, and of not having a system that evaluates preservice teachers once ensconced in their own classrooms (Easton, Education Department's Reform Plan for Teacher Training Gets Mixed Reviews, 2011). How educators meet this challenge to give students the skills to teach differently in their own classrooms while cultivating complexity and curiosity in courses is a predicament educators may choose to confront in various ways.

Teaching history to students who may display little open interest is both a challenge and an opportunity to change attitudes about the role and purpose of education in the lives of students. One of the first aspects of good teaching is knowing that you are not teaching a discipline. You are teaching people, and as with any encounter first impressions matter. Knowing who you are teaching will often give you a head start. Show that you respect the cultural values, mores and knowledge that students of color bring to the classroom.

Before we can respect these students, we must recognize and acknowledge their funds of knowledge. There is almost no valid excuse for people living in the twenty-first century not to be able to find out about other cultures. The technology age has given us copious information and search engines that claim to make sense out of the babble and cacophony of data the World

Wide Web spits out. Learning is a two-way street and you should be willing and perceptive enough to learn from your students of color and their families. Community engagement and having more than a surface understanding of the students you teach is essential.

People in general like talking about themselves, so educators need to tap into this and make use of the information gleamed. Your history classroom environment should reflect the children that you teach, in classroom furniture, strategies and methods. It should be a place where people can learn that being different is not wrong, just different.

> I have had a tumultuous past with history classes. The extent of learning typically consisted of a last-minute cram session followed by a trained regurgitation of dates and details that left my brain the moment I finished the exams. I couldn't understand the current day value of learning about history. However, two ideas from this class broke this notion, broadened my scope and finally allowed me to see the history's relevance (Laura 22).

Conclusion

This brief outline of some techniques that work in a class of diverse students in terms of age, gender, racial identities, and experiences demonstrates the necessity of teachers supplying a level of instruction that does not undermine students' perceptions of choice and control and creates a sense of ownership and belonging in the classroom. These strategies create a sense of community in a short time as all students focus and engage in uncovering the past to make sense of the present.

Over three decades ago, the author wrote what follows in this conclusion. Rereading still seems relevant.

Why is history still taught in schools? What is it about this subject that engenders so much debate, and why do history teachers constantly feel the need to justify their subject?

History in education should seek to develop in students the understanding that they are part of a wider society. History in education should deal with the individuality of situations, the choices made, the motivations behind those choices and the outcomes. History in education needs to develop in students an understanding of these choices, thereby causing students to see that they can actively take part in shaping history.

Students gain and test their values by weighing up the past and the present. The present can only be properly understood in the context of the past. Just a quick glance at our daily newspapers makes that abundantly clear.

Students can only begin to understand the societies in which they live by understanding the history. By studying the past students can perhaps more fully understand cause and consequence and how to cope with change when it occurs. They also may learn to appreciate or better understand their society and its institutions and how and why they function as they do. It is through history that educators can develop in students understanding, sensitivity, and an appreciation of life circumstances in both the past and the present.

School history should try to teach students to understand the past. It is essential to teach an appreciation of the diversity and value of various cultures and lifestyles if we want our students to function in diverse societies. We cannot afford to be limited and blind in our history teaching. We cannot afford to tack on areas of world history as an appendage to the rise of the West and "exceptionalism." The frequent failure to respond to cultural diversity in the classroom is a major cause of criticism from many marginalized groups. The study of history can and needs to at least try to address this.

The study of history may better enable students to understand the concept of change and how people coped with it. They need to learn that change is sometimes unwelcome, it is not always for the best, but often inevitable. Knowing that change is not constant and, at times, seems to move rapidly and, at other times, at a snail's pace may help answer some of their questions about the present. History is probably the only subject on the timetable that considers in detail religious, ideological, social, political and economic factors and their effects on different societies.

History lessons should try to teach students the process of decision making through problem-based lessons that help students see how people in the past have dealt with complex issues, and that decisions are not always easy and may have to be defended and adhered to, or fought against. It is alright to change your mind in light of compelling new evidence. By examining people of the past, students learn what they can do, and perhaps what they do not want to do. They may come to value their own uniqueness as well as that of other people. Studying history, they may not agree with historical figures, but perhaps they can better understand those who fight for justice and learn that individual people may make a difference.

History lessons often teach intentional and unintentional values to all our students. Examining aspects of the past may help students question some values as well as clarify, and affirm others. Studying history, it is possible for students to learn skills of inquiry, integrity, and justice. They may habitually come to distinguish between the motives and feelings of people, and empathize with predicaments people in the past encountered, even if they do not agree with them. And perhaps students may start to make connections with the present and begin to have answers to some of their questions.

Rich learning environments are said by research to start with effective educators taking responsibility for the climates they produce (Ayers, 1993). Research into classroom climate has long claimed that the nature of school and classroom environments has a significant effect both on teacher satisfaction and how well students achieve. Furthermore, students' involvement often stems from being able to work in groups, taking on more responsibility for their learning, and having teachers value their efforts.

In creating classroom environments, which are more likely to cater for affective concerns, brain-based educational research has long suggested strategies. Once people thought brains were hard-wired and that they could not be changed. Now it is claimed that positive environments can produce physical changes in the brain (Jensen, 1998, p. 46). Heredity gives about 30 to 60 per cent of the brain's wiring, and 40 to 70 per cent is from the effect of the environment (Jenson, 1998). If, as educators we take just this aspect that nurturing the environments of students can make a significant difference to the development of their brains, the possibilities for improving learning for all students appear staggering.

Might an environment which allows for more personal history inclusion create better learning? "When we enrich the environment, we get brains with a thicker cortex, more dendritic branching, more growth spines and larger cell bodies" (Healy, 1990, p. 47). It appears that IQ measurements are possibly changed as much as 20 points up or down, based on environment. This research seems to suggest educators need to pay much more attention to workings of the brain. This includes affective factors, if they are attempting to maximize the interest and learning potentials of their students.

As educators we are doing some of this by providing and encouraging students to become more actively engaged in their learning and in guiding their own instruction, and when possible giving students more choice in what they study. The goal of most educators is to teach for understanding, application, and mastery and meaning, and to create learning environments that are frequently high in challenge and low in threat. It may follow that creating more comfortable learning environments through more inclusive history curricula and teaching strategies based on scientific findings can create better learning opportunities in classrooms for all students.

In conclusion, perhaps one of the most fundamental questions history educators need to be asking themselves is:

What kind of world will we probably be sharing twenty years from now?

Cultivating Curiosity, Complexity and Authentic Engagement   139

When the author first asked this questions, 9/11 had not happened. But in the twenty-first century it is still relevant to ask the following. What histories or skills will our students probably need to know in the next twenty years? How do we develop the attributes of lifelong learning within our students? Are history curricula in the present guises developing students more likely to participate and engage in democratic societies? Are our history lessons developing better thinkers and not mere reflectors of the thoughts of others? Do our students have a love of learning?

As a history teacher, the author has always shied away from making predictions, preferring to investigate the past. However, the educational trends of the last twenty years and contemporary events enable suggestions that the following three factors are probably inevitable:

1. The global village will probably become even smaller and more interconnected.
2. The continuing increase in technology will probably create more innovative ways to capture the interest of learners.
3. Science will probably continue to unravel the mysteries of how and why we learn and suggest methods to improve teaching.

All three of the above are mingled with probable opportunities, challenges, and threats. How we as educators choose to engage in the challenges they present will often impact in some way on future generations. To teach as well as we possibly can is a demanding responsibility, and to introduce and engage all students to the wonders, mysteries and problems involved in exploring the past an ambitious goal. We may need to explore as many avenues as possible to help maximize positive learning outcomes for all our students.

This book attempted in a limited way to report what students have been saying for over twenty years. There are no easy answers to the issues they raise. The author, however, is still convinced that effective concerns within the history classroom are important now and will probably become even more salient as we move further into the twenty-first century.

History is a discipline driven by questions, and a subject which can help answer some of our own questions about the past, present, and, perhaps, the future. However, it is clear in the last thirty years history lessons and personal experiences jarred. History lessons did not adequately answer questions students of color had about race and racism in the past, or the present, nor perhaps can history lessons ever do so.

In the United States, race is a significant mediating factor for students of color, so it is not surprising the topic students of color had most questions about was the issue of slavery, and why racism was and is still so acceptable. The question that Faith asks is repeated often in the reflections from students of color:

> The question I would like to know would be "when will racism end"? Although that is a question I wish I could write about, unfortunately I do not have an answer (Faith, African American, female).

As history teachers we too have no clear answer to this question. However, giving students a safe place and the opportunity to debate the history of racism entwined in attitudes and actions of the past and present is important. Racism has left indelible fingerprints on the present that probably stretch into the future and make it an issue that as educators we should not choose to repress or ignore.

The implications of this book for teaching and learning of history in schools are many. First and foremost, evidence from the voices of the students of color indicates that educators may need greater awareness of the ideas and prior conceptions these students bring to the history classroom. These include cognitive and emotional conceptions about what these students think history is for. A better understanding of the informal versions of history that students may bring to the classroom will enable us to improve the tailoring of the formal curriculum that we have to offer. Second, there is the need to put more effort into getting students of color to see the importance of the discipline in answering their questions.

We need to work toward improving the abilities of students of color to engage in analytical thought processes about formal and informal history learning, to evaluate all versions of the past critically and comfortably. This does not mean ignoring unpleasant issues, but it may mean trying to be more sensitive to the impact that our attitudes or turn of phrase toward people of color may have on all the children we teach. It does mean striving toward building a conceptual framework that enables all our students to gain a firm grasp of history as a discipline. We need to help them understand what pictures of the past are by giving them a firm conceptual framework to work from and to guide them. We need to help them develop skills that enable them to arrange, retrieve and apply knowledge (Bransford et al., 1999).

It may mean trying to find out about the multiple identities that children bring to the classroom in order to work toward identifying and challenging misconceptions. Above all it means trying to understand both how our students think and how our students feel.

Appendix

Data Collection, Coding and Method of Analysis for Counterstories in Chapter 7

The reflections were analyzed with the qualitative method of narrative inquiry. Narrative inquiry is analysis, explication, and explanation, and students' reflections could be explored, provoked, and interpreted to sift through layers of meaning inherent in their storylines (Czarnawska, 2004).

Qualitative analysis involved close reading and theming of the data (Saldana, 2009). Comparing narratives, looking for similarities, differences and seeing patterns, and then finding categories and eventually general themes emerging was rewarding (Ezzy, 2002). Students' reflections were analyzed collectively and then separately. The categories emerged from a holistic review of all student comments. Students often self-indicated racial affiliation during reflections.

Category Coding

Interrogating the reflections involved searching for funds of knowledge and taking ideas as the smallest meaningful element in any part of a sentence. A holistic reviewing of all the students' comments uncovered several similarities and differences, which began emerging between often self-identifying students of color and White students. Clear themes began emerging, including, sports, gender issues, social justice aspects, leaders, and conflicts. Establishing inductive categories from these themes led to four main categories.

Describing, analyzing, comparing, and evaluating the data from students of color and White students was the main focus of the study.

Categories and Indicators

1. *Understanding the contemporary*—the student makes mention of the present and a direct relationship with the past: "It seems that people's beliefs and actions still live on in the mindset that African Americans are not equal and will never be equal."
2. *Learning lessons*—The student reasons that history helps people learn lessons and avoid making errors by showing "what, why, and how" things happened in the past, and makes direct mention of learning from the past: "History should help us from repeating similar mistakes and help us learn from them."
3. *Direction of change as progress or deterioration*[1]—The student makes value judgments about the past, compares it with the present and mentions the deficit of the past and the plusses of the present. The student makes value judgments about the past and sees change as an inevitable process in terms of progression and/or deterioration: "Although slavery has ended for the United States a long time ago, some beliefs still live on in the world of racism."
4. *Ownership*—The student refers to a personal attachment to a history, uses personal pronouns to express an attachment to a history, country, or culture, or makes favorable comparison or uses possessive figures of speech to describe people or culture: "I found slavery in the Caribbean Islands interesting because my family is from the Caribbean."

Note

1. There were differences in statements made by minority and White students concerning the directionality of change, hence the combing of "progress" and "deterioration."

References

Alexander, C. & Weekes-Bernard, D. (2017). History lessons: inequality, diversity and the national curriculum. *Race Ethnicity and Education*, 20(4), 478–494.

Anderson, B. R. O. G. (1991). *Imagined communities: Reflections on the origin and spread of nationalism*. London: Verso.

Anderson, C. A., & Jennings, D. L. (1980). When Experiences of Failure Promote Expectations of Success. *Journal of Personality*, 48(3), 393–403.

Angharad E. Beckett (2009) 'Challenging disabling attitudes, building an inclusive society': considering the role of education in encouraging non-disabled children to develop positive attitudes towards disabled people, British Journal of Sociology of Education, 30:3, 317-329, DOI: 10.1080/01425690902812596.

Archer, S. (1994). Interventions for adolescent identity development (pp.12–13). London: Sage.

Arnesen, E. (2003). *Black protest and the great migration*. Boston: Bedford St. Martin's.

Asante, M. K. (1991/1992). "Afrocentric Curriculum." *Educational Leadership* 49: 28–31.

Asher, N. (2007). Made in the (Multicultural) U.S.A.: Unpacking Tensions of Race, Culture, Gender, and Sexuality in Education. *Educational Researcher*, 36(2), 65–73.

Association of American Educators Foundation (2019) https://www.aaeadvocacy.org/aaef-letter-on-teacher-diversity aaeteachers.org/diversity.

Atkinson, J. W. (1957). Motivational determinants of risk-taking behavior. *Psychological Review*, 64(6), 359–372.

Ayers, W. (1993). *To teach: The journey of a teacher*. London: Teacher College Press.

Bandura, A. (1977). *Social learning theory*. Englewood Cliffs: Prentice-Hall.

Bandura, A. (1985). *Social foundations of thought and action*. New Jersey: Prentice Hall.

Banks, J. A. (1991) Social studies, ethnic diversity and social change. In C. V. Willie, A. M. Garibaldi & W. L. Reed (Eds.) *The education of African-Americans*. pp. 129–147. Boston: Auburn House.

Barca Oliveira, M. I. (1996). Adolescent students' ideas about provisional historical explanation. Unpublished doctoral thesis. University of London, Institute of Education. London, U.K.

Barton, K. C. (1996). Narrative simplifications in elementary students' historical thinking. *Advances in Research on Teaching, 6*, 51–83.

Barton, K. C., & Levstik, L. S. (2004). *Teaching history for the common good*. London: Lawrence Erlbaum Associates.

Biggs, J. (2003). *Teaching for quality learning at university*. Philadelphia: SHRE and Open University Press.

Bills, R. E., Vance, E. L., & McClean, O. S. (1951). An index of adjustment and values. *Journal of Consulting Psychology, 15(3)*, 257–261.

Boje, D. (2008). *Storytelling in organization*. CA: Sage Publications Inc.

Bonilla-Silva, E. (2010). *Racism without racists*. New York: Rowman & Littlefield Publishers, INC.

Bransford, J. D., et al., (1999). *How people learn*. Washington D.C: National Academy Press.

Brogan, H. (1985). *The Penguin history of the United States of American*. London: Penguin books.

Bruner, J. (1991). The narrative construction of reality. *Critical Inquiry, 18(1)*, 1–21. https://www.jstor.org/stable/1343711.

Bullock, H. A. (1967). *A history of Negro Education in the South: From 1619 to the Present*. Cambridge, MA: Harvard University Press.

Burke, E., Christian, D., Dunn, R. E. (2012). *World history the big eras: A compact history of humankind for teachers and students*. Culver City CA: Social Studies School Service.

Burr, V. (2003). *Social constructionism*. New York: Routledge.

Caine, R. N., & Caine, G. (1994). *Making connections: Teaching and the human brain*. California: Addison-Wesley.

Clandinin, D. J. & Conenelly, F. M. (2000). *Narrative inquiry: Experience and story in qualitative research*. San Francisco: Jossey Bass.

Clark, K. B. (1971). *Crisis in urban education*. Vermont: Middlebury College.

Coleman Report (1966). *Washington D. C.: U.S. Government Printing Office*. Retrieved from https//files.eric.ed.gov/fulltext/ED012275.pdf.

Covington, M. V. (1992). *Making the grade*. Cambridge: Cambridge University Press.

Czarniawska, B. (2004). *Narratives in social science research*. London: Sage Publications Ltd.

Danticat, E. (1995). *Krik? Krak!* New York: Vintage Books.

Deci, E., & Ryan, R. (2000). *Intrinsic motivation and self-determination in human behavior*. New York: Plenum Press.

Delany, M. R. (1966). "The condition, elevation, emigration and the Destiny of the colored people of the United States." *In Negro social and Political Thought, 1850–1920: Representative Texts.* Ed. H. Brotz. New York: Basic Books Inc.

Delgado, R. (1995). Legal storytelling: Storytelling for oppositionists and others: A pleas for narrative. In R. Delgado (Ed.), *Critical race theory: The cutting edge.* Philadelphia: Temple University Press.

Dentler, R. A. (1991). School desegregation since Gunnar Myrdal's American Dilemma. In C. V. Willie, A. M. Garibaldi & W. L. Reed. (Eds.). *The education of African-Americans.* Pp. 27–50. New York: Auburn House.

Diamond, M., & Hopson, J. (1998). *Magic trees of the mind.* New York: Dutton Books.

Douglass, F. (1845). *Narrative of the life of Frederick Douglass an American slave.* Antislavery office. Boston.

Du Bois, W. E. B. (1968).*The souls of black folk; essays and sketches. Chicago, A. G. McClurg, 1903.* New York:Johnson Reprint Corp.

Dudziak, M. L. (2009). "Desegregation as Cold War imperative." In Foundations of Critical Race Theory in Education. Eds. E. Taylor, D. Gillborn, and G. Ladson-Billings. New York: Routledge.

Dunning, W. A. (1907). *Reconstruction, political and economic, 1865–1877.* New York: Harper and Bros.

Easton, C. (2011, October 2). Education department's reform plan for teacher training gets mixed reviews. Retrieved from *The Chronicle of Higher Education*: http://chronicle.com/article/Education-Depts-Reform-Plan/129258/.

Eco, U., (2003). *Baudolino, Florida*: Harcourt, 2003.

Edgington, D. (Ed.). (1982). *Occasional papers IV extramural division.* London: SOAS University of London.

Education, 21(5), 573–592.

Eiser, J. (1986). *Social Psychology: Attitudes, cognition and social behaviour.* Cambridge: Cambridge University Press.

El-Haj, T.R.A. (2006). *Elusive justice: Wrestling with difference and educational equity in everyday practice.* New York. Routledge.

Emdin, C. (2016). *For White Folks Who Teach in the Hood…and the Rest of Y"all Too. Reality Pedagogy and Urban Education.* Boston: Beacon Press.

Entwistle, N. J. (1987). *Understanding classroom learning.* London: Hodder & Stoughton.

Epstein, T. L. (1993). Multiculturalism and the politics of history: A response to Thomas Sobol. *Teachers College Record, 95,* (2), 273–282.

Epstein, T. L. (1997). Sociocultural approaches to young people's historical understanding. *Social Education, 61,* (1), 28–31.

Erikson, E. H. (1968). *Identity youth and crisis.* New York: Norton.

Ezzy, D. (2002). *Qualitative analysis: Practice and innovation.* London: Routledge.

Fallace, T. (2012.) Recapitulation theory and the new Eeducation: Race, culture, imperialism, and pedagogy, 1894–1916. *Curriculum Inquiry, 42*(4), 510–533.

Feistritzer, C.M. (2011). *Profile of teachers in the U.S, 2011*.Washington D.C.: National Center for Education Information.

Feldman, M. S., Skoldberg, K. & Brown, R. N. (2004). Making sense of stories: A rhetorical approach to narrative analysis. *Journal of public administration research and theory, 14 (2)*, 147–170.

Fisher, D. R. (1972). Black studies and the enhancement of self-concept as it relates to achievement in negro high school students. Dissertation abstracts, 1972 (A). 5468. In A. Harris Stoddard, (1975). *The effects of integrated history materials on black secondary students*. Unpublished master's thesis. University of Georgia, Athens: Georgia, USA.

Fraser, B. (1986) *Classroom environment*. London: Croom Helm.

Freire, P. (1970) *Pedagogy of the oppressed*. New York: Continuum.

Garcia, T., & Pintrich, P. (1995). *The role of possible selves in adolescents' perceived competence and self-regulation*. (ERIC Documentation Reproduction Service No. ED386437).

Gay, G. (2010). *Culturally responsive teaching: Theory, research, and practice (2nd Ed.)*. New York: Teachers College Press.

Gilroy, P. (1987). *There ain't no black in the Union Jack: The culture of politics and race*. London: Routledge.

Good, T. L., & Brophy, J. E. (2007). *Looking in classrooms*. New York: Harper & Row.

Grant, C. (2008). *Negro with a hat: The rise and fall of Marcus Garvey*. New York: Oxford University Press.

Greenwald, A. G., & Pratkanis, A. R. (1988). The self. In Wyer, R. S., & Srull, T. K., (Eds.). *Handbook of Social Cognition*: Vol. 3. Hillsdale: Earlbaum.

Greven, P. J. R. (1984). Entertaining Satan. In *History and Theory*, 23, (2), 236–251.

Griffiths, M., & Macleod, G. (2008). Personal narratives and policy: Never the twain? *Journal of Philosophy and Education*, 42(1), 121–142. https://doi.org/10.1111/j.1467-9752.2008.00632.x.

Gubrium, J. F., & Holstein, J. A. (2009). *Analyzing narrative reality*. Thousand Oaks, CA: Sage.

Haenen, J., & Tuithof, H. (2008). Cooperative learning: The place of pupil involvement in a history textbook. *Teaching History, 131*, 30–34.

Haenen, J., & Tuithof, H. (2008). Cooperative Learning: The place of pupil involvement in a history textbook. *Teaching History*, 30–34.

Hale-Benson, J. H. (1986). *Black Children: Their roots and culture, and learning styles*. Rev. ed. Baltimore, MD: Johns Hopkins University Press.

Hall, E. T. (1977). *Beyond culture*. New York: Anchor.

Healy, J. (1990). *Endangered minds: Why our children can't think*. New York: Doubleday.

Henderson, A. T. & Mapp, K.L. (2002). *A new wave of evidence: The impact of school, family, and community on student achievement*. Austin, Texas: National Center for Family and Community Connections with Schools.

Herrnstein, R. J. Murray, C. (1994). *The bell curve: Intelligence and class structure in American life*. New York: Free Press.

Hollins, C. & Govan, I. (2015). *Diversity, Equity and Inclusion: Strategies for facilitating conversations on race.* New York: Rowman and Littlefield.

Hooks, b. (1994). *Teaching to transgress.* New York: Routledge.

Hughes, R. L. (2007). A hint of whiteness: History textbooks and social construction of race in the wake of the sixties. *Social Studies* (Sept/Oct), 201–207.

Hurston, Z. N. (1937). *Their eyes were watching god.* New York: Harper Perennial.

Jackson, C. L. (2001). *African American Education: A Reference handbook.* Santa Barbara, California: ABC CLIO.

Jackson, D. H. (2008). Booker T. Washington and the Struggle against White Supremacy: The Southern Educational Tours, 1908–1912. New York City, NY: Palgrave Macmillan.

James, G. G. M. (1954)1989. Stolen legacy. Reprint, New York: United Brother Communications Systems.

Jensen, E. (1998). *Teaching with the brain in mind.* Alexandria, VA: Association for Supervision and Curriculum Development.

Kincaid, J. (1985). *Annie John.* New York: Farrar, Strauss and Giroux.

King, J. E. & Swartz, E. E. (2018) *Heritage knowledge in the curriculum: Retrieving an African episteme.* New York, NY: Routledge.

Kozol, J. (1992). *Savage inequalities: Children in American schools.* New York NY: Harper Perennial.

Kymlicka, W. (2012). *Multiculturalism: Success, Failure, and the Future.* Washington D.C: Migration Policy Institute.

Ladson-Billings, G. (1994). *The dream keepers: Successful teachers of African American children.* San Francisco. Jossey-Bass.

Ladson-Billings, G. (2000). Fighting for our lives: Preparing teachers to teach African American students. *Journal of Teacher Education, 51* (3), 206–214.

Lee, C. D., & Slaughter-Defoe, D. T. (2003). Historical and sociocultural influences on African American education. In J. A. Banks., & C. A. McGee-Banks, (Eds.), *Handbook of research on multicultural education* (pp. 348–371). London: Macmillan.

Lee, P. J. (1995). History and the National Curriculum in England. In A. Dickinson, P. Gordon, P. Lee., & J. Slater (Eds.), *International yearbook of history education.* London: Woburn Press.

Lee, P. J., & Ashby, R. (1987). Discussing the evidence. *Teaching History, 48,* 13–17.

Lee, P. J., & Ashby, R. (2001). Empathy, perspective taking, and rational understanding. In O. L Davis J. R., S. Foster., & E. Yaeger, (Eds.), *Historical empathy and perspective taking in social studies.* London: Rowman & Littlefield.

Levstik, L. S (2000). Articulating the silences: teachers and adolescents conceptions of historical significance. In P. N. Stearns, P. Seixas., and S. Wineburg, (eds.), *Knowing teaching and learning history* (pp. 284–305). London: New York University Press.

Lewin, K. (1948). *Resolving social conflicts; Selected papers on group dynamics.* G.W. Lewin (Ed.). New York: Harper & Row.

Lewis, C. W. Chambers, T. V. & Butler, B. R. (2012). Urban Education in the 21st Century: An Overview of Selected Issues That Impact African American Student Outcomes. In J.L. Moore III, and C. W. Lewis (eds.), *African American students in urban schools: Critical issues and solutions for achievement*. New York: Peter Lang.

Lowenthal, D. (1985). *The past is a foreign country*. Cambridge Cambridgeshire: Cambridge University Press.

Lustig, M.W., & Koester, J., (2013). *Intercultural competence: interpersonal communication across cultures*. 7th ed. Boston: Pearson.

Lyotard, J. F. (1984). *The postmodern condition: A report on knowledge*. (G. Bennington & B. Massumi, Trans.). Minneapolis, MN: University of Minnesota Press.

Malcolm, X. (1964) 1999. *The autobiography of Malcolm X*. As told to Alex Haley. New York: Ballantine Books.

Marcus, A. S., Metzger, S. A., Paxton, R. J., & Stoddard, J. D. (2010). *Teaching history with Film: Strategies for secondary social studies*. New York, NY: Routledge.

Marks, R. (2007). *The origins of the modern world: A global and ecological narrative* (2nd Ed.). Maryland: Rowman and Littlefield Publishers Inc.

Markus, H. R., & Kitayama, S. (1991). Culture and the self: Implications for cognition, emotion, and motivation. *Psychological Review*, 98(2), 224–253.

Marshall, P. (1983). *Reena, and other stories*. New York: The Feminist Press.

Marton, F., & Salijo, R. (1984). Approaches to learning. In P. Horton, D. Hounsell, & N. Entwistle (Ed.).*The Experience of Learning* (pp. 39–44). Edinburgh: Scottish Academic Press.

Mbiti, J. S. (1970). *African religions and philosophy*. New York: Anchor.

McAdams, D. (1993). *The stories we live by: Personal myths and the making of the self*. New York, NY: Guildford.

McCarthy, C. (1994). After the canon: Knowledge and ideological representation in the multicultural discourse on curriculum reform. In C. McCarthy., & W. Crichlow, (Eds.), *Race identity and representation in education* (pp. 289–305). London: Routledge.

McDonald, J. L. Jessell, J. C. (1992). Influence of selected variables on occupational attitudes and perceived occupational abilities of young adolescents. *Journal of Career Development* vol 18. No. 4. 239–250.

McGlynn, A. P. (2001). *Successful beginnings for college teaching* (Teaching Techniques/Strategies Series, V. 2). Madison WI: Atwood Publishing.

Miller, H. (2012). *Governing narratives*. Tuscaloosa, AL: The University of Alabama Press.

Millis, B. J. & Cottell, P. G. (1998). *Cooperative learning for higher education faculty*. Phoenix, Arizona: American Council on Education Oryx Press.

Milner, H. (1956). Body ritual among the Nacirema. *American Anthropologist*, 58 (3), 503–507.

Moll, L. C., Amanti, C. Neff, D. & Gonzalez, N. (1992). Funds of Knowledge for teaching: Using a qualitative approach to connect homes and classrooms. *Theory into Practice (31)*, 132–141.

Montgomery, K. C. (1954). *The role of exploratory drive in learning. Journal of comparative psychology in learning, 47(1)*, 60–64.

Moynihan, P. (1965). *The Negro family: The case for action.* Washington D.C.: Office of Planning and Research, United States Department of Labor.

Munson, W. (1992) 'Self-esteem, vocational identity, and career salience in high school students.' *Career Development Quarterly* Vol 40 N0 4.: 361–68, June 1992. ERIC.

Myrdal, G. (1962) 1944. *An American dilemma: The Negro problem and modern democracy.* 6th edition. New York: Harper & Row.

Nathan, R. (2006). *My freshman year: What a professor learned by becoming a student.* New York: Penguin Books.

National Assessment of Educational Progress, NAEP. (2014). Retrieved from https://nces.ed.gov/nationsreportcard/.

National Center for Educational Statistics, NCES. (2016). Retrieved from https://nces.ed.gov/fastfacts/display.asp?id=16.

Neal, L.I., McCray, A.D., Webb-Johnson, G., & Bridgest, S.T. (2003). The effects of African American movement styles on teachers' perceptions and reactions. *Journal of Special Education, (37)*, 49–57.

Nelson, J. L. and Ooka Pang, V. (2014). Prejudice, racism and the Social Studies curriculum. In Ross, E. W. (Ed) *Social Studies curriculum, the fourth edition: Purposes, problems and possibilities.* Pp. 139–153. Ebook High School Collection (EBSCOhost))-printed on 5/31/2019.

Nobles, W. (1992). *Standing in the river: African (black) psychology transformed and transforming.* London: Karia Press.

Norrell, R. J. (2011). *Up from History: The Life of Booker T. Washington.* Cambridge MA: the Belnap Press of Harvard University Press.

Ogbu, J. U. (1995). Understanding cultural diversity and learning. In J. A. Banks., & C. A. McGee-Banks, (Eds.), *Handbook of research on multicultural education* (pp. 582–593). London: Macmillan.

Omni, M., & Winant, H. (1991) By the Rivers of Babylon: Race in the United States. In *Socialist Review* (Ed.), Unfinished Business 20 Years of Socialist Review. Chicago: Haymarket.

Oyserman, D., & Markus, H. (1990). Possible selves in balance: Implications for delinquency. *Journal of Social Issues, 46 (2)*, 141–157.

Pandey, G. (2013). *A history of race and prejudice: Race, cast, and difference in India and the United States.* New York: Cambridge University Press.

Paris, E. (2000). *Long shadows.* London: Bloomsbury Publishing Plc.

Patel, K. (1994). *Multicultural education in all white areas.* Aldershot: Avebury.

Penuel, W. R., and Wertsch, J. V. (1998). Historical representation as mediated action: official history as a tool. In James, F. Voss., and M. Carretero, (Eds.), *International Review of History Education (2)*, 23–38. London: Woburn Press.

Pierce, C. (1970). Offensive mechanisms. In F. Barbour (Ed.), *The Black seventies* (pp. 265–282). Boston, MA: Porter Sargent.

Ramsden, P. (1992). *Learning to teach in Higher Education*. London: Routledge.
Ravitch, D. (1983).*The troubled crusade: American education 1945–1980*. New York: Basic Books.
Richert, A. E., Donahue, D. M., & LaBoskey, V. K. (2009). Preparing white teachers to teach in a racist nation: What do they need to know and be able to do? In *The handbook of Social Justice in Education*. W. Ayers, T. Quinn, D. Stovall (Eds.), New York: Routledge.
Riessman, F. (1962). *The culturally deprived child*. New York: Basic Books.
Rogers, C. R. (1989). *Selections*. Boston: Houghton Mifflin.
Rogers, T. B., Kuiper, N. A., & Kirker, W. S. (1977). Self-reference and the encoding of personal information. *Journal of Personality and Social Psychology, 35*, 677–688.
Rosenberg, M. (1965). *Society and the adolescent self-image*. New Jersey: Princeton University Press.
Rubie-Davis, C. M. (2007). Classroom interactions: Exploring the practices of high- and low-expectation teachers. *British journal of Educational Psychology, 77(2)*, 289–306.
Rüsen, J. (1993). *Studies in meta history*, Duvenage (Ed.). Pretoria: Human Sciences Research Council.
Rüsen, J. (2004). *Theorizing historical consciousness*, Seixas (Ed.). Toronto: University of Toronto Press.
Ryan, R. & Deci, E. (2000). "Intrinsic and Extrinsic Motivations: Classic Definitions and New Directions' *Contemporary Educational Psychology, (25)*, 54–67.
Said, E. (1993).The politics of knowledge. In *Race identity and representation in education*. C. McCarthy & W. Crichlow (Eds.). Pp.306–314. London: Routledge.
Saldana, J. (2009). *The coding manual for qualitative researchers*. London: Routledge.
Sampson, E. E. (1993). Identity politics challenges to psychology's understanding. *American Psychologist, (48)*, 1219–1230.
Sapon-Shevin, M. (2007). *Widening the Circle: The power of inclusive classrooms*. Boston, Massachusetts: Beacon Press.
Schlecty, P. (1994). Increasing student leadership. In *Educational Leadership, 51*, 8.
School and Staffing Survey, SSS. (2011). *National center for education*. Retrieved from https://nces.ed.gov/surveys/sass/.
Seuss, Dr. (1953). *The Sneetches and other stories*. New York: Penguin Random House LLC.
Shemilt, D. (1980). *History, 13–16 evaluation study*. Edinburgh: Holmes McDougall.
Showstack, E. (2012). Symbolic power in the heritage language classroom: How Spanish heritage speakers sustain and resist hegemonic discourses on languages and cultural diversity. *Spanish in Context, 9(1)*, 1–26.
Simon, D. (2005). Education of the blacks: the supplementary school movement. In B. Richardson (Ed.),*Tell it like it is: How our schools fail black children*. London: Bookmarks Publications.
Sire, J. W. (1997). *The universe next door*. (3rd ed). Leicester: Intervarsity Press.

Sleeter, C. E. (2011). The academic and social value of ethnic studies: A research review. *National Education Association*. Retrieved from http://www.nea.org/assets/docs/NBI-2010-3-value-of-ethnic-studies.pdf.

Snyder, B. R. (1971). *The hidden curriculum*. Massachusetts: Massachusetts Institute of Technology.

Sue, D. W., Capodilupo, C.M., Torino, G. C., Bucceri, J., Holder, A.M. B., Nadal, K.L., and Esquilin, M. (2007). Racial migroagressions in everyday life: Implications for clinical practice. *American Psychologist, 62*(4), 271–86.

Tajfel, H. (1981). *Human groups and social categories: Studies in social psychology*. Cambridge: Cambridge University Press.

Tashlin, F. (2007). *The bear that wasn't*. New York: Dover Publications.

Tatum, B. D. (1997). *Why are all the black kids sitting together in the cafeteria?* New York: Basic Books.

Taylor, E. Gillborn, D., & Ladson-Billings, G.(eds.). (2009). *Foundations of Critical Race Theory in Education*. New York: Routledge.

Tuten, J. H. (2010). *Low country time and tide: The fall of the South Carolina rice kingdom*. Columbia, South Carolina: University of South Carolina Press.

Volz, A. Higdon, J. & Lidwell, W. (2019). *The elements of Education for Teachers: 50 Research-Based Principles Every Educator Should Know*. New York, NY: Routledge.

Walsh, P. (1992). History and love of the past. In P. Lee, D. Shemilt, J. Slater, P. Walsh., & J. White. *The aims of school history: The national curriculum and beyond* (pp. 35–44). London: The Tufnell Press.

Washington, B. T. (1901).*Up from slavery*. W. F. Brundage, (Ed.), Boston: Bedford St. Martins.

Washington, B. T. (1968). *The future of the American Negro*. New York: Haskell.

Weber, A. L. (1992). *Social psychology*. New York: Harper Collins.

Weber, R. P. (1990). *Basic content analysis* (2nd ed.). London: Sage.

Weinberg, M. (1991). The civil rights movement and educational change. In C. V. Willie, A. M. Garibaldi & W. L. Reed (Eds.). *The education of African-Americans*. Boston: Auburn House.

Weiner, B. (1972). *Theories of motivation: From mechanism to cognition*. Chicago: Markham.

Weiner, B. (1972). *Theories of motivation: From mechanism to cognition*. Chicago: Markham.

Weinstein, Y. Sumeracki, M. & Caviglioli, O. (2019). *Understanding how we learn: A visual guide*. New York, NY: Routledge.

Wertsch, J. V. (1994). Struggling with the past: Some dynamics of historical representation. In M. Carretero., & J. F. Voss, (Eds.), *Cognitive and instructional processes in history and the social sciences* (pp. 323–338). Hove, UK: Lawrence Erlbaum Associates.

Williams, H. A. (2005). *Self-taught: African American education in slavery and freedom*. Chapel Hill: University of North Carolina.

Wilson, M. D. (1985). *History for pupils with learning difficulties*. London: Hodder & Stoughton.

Wineburg, S. (2000). Making historical sense. In P. N. Stearns, P. Seixas., & S. Wineburg. *Knowing teaching and learning history*. London: New York University Press.

Wineburg, S. (2000). Making historical sense. In P. N. Stearns, P. Seixas., & S. Wineburg. *Knowing Teaching and Learning History*. London: New York University Press.

Wineburg, S. (2001). *Historical thinking and other unnatural acts: Charting the future of teaching the Past* (Critical perspectives on the Past). Philadelphia: Temple University Press.

Wood, P.H. (1974). *Black Majority: Negroes in colonial South Carolina from 1670 through the Stono rebellion*. New York: W.W. Norton & Company.

Woodson, C. G. (1933) 1991. *The Mis-Education of the Negro*. Reprint. Philadelphia: Hamik's Publications.

Zeichner, K. (2016). Advancing social justice and democracy in teacher education: Teacher Preparation 1.0, 2.0, and 3.0. *Kappa Delta Pi Record, 52(4)*. 150–155.

Zeringue, J. T. (2015) "Booker T. Washington and the Historians: How Changing Views on Race Relations, Economics, and Education Shaped Washington Historiography, 1915–2010" (2015). LSU Master's Theses. 1154. https://digitalcommons.lsu.edu/gradschool_theses/1154.

Zwiers, J. (2008). *Building academic language: Essential practices for content classrooms, grades 5–12*. San Francisco: Jossey-Bass.

Index

Aborigines, 75
academic underperformance, 10
accountability, 13
achievement, 52, 63
action, 18, 46–48
activities, 74, 77; activity-classroom climate, 119–20; collaborative instruction and, 132–33; new competencies and, 123–24
adaptations, xiii
Adequate Yearly Progress (AYP), 13
Adichie, Chimamanda, 125–26
adolescence, 38, 44
affective factors, 29–44
African Americans, 85; citizenship and, 6; history education for, 1–16; history lessons and, 22–23; jockeys as, 123; share-cropping and, 90
African Diaspora, 37, 127
African National Congress (ANC), 74
Afrocentric narratives, 23–25
age, 34–35, 77
agency, 7; narrative method and, 78
alienation, 61; history lessons and, 68
alternative histories, 19

alternative narratives, 17, 105–7
American Dilemma (Myrdal), 16
American History, 73–93
ANC. *See* African National Congress
ancestors, 61
anecdotes, 100
anger, 53, 77; engagement and, 66; experience and, 71; history lessons and, 63
apartheid, 74–75, 106
approach, 42; to teaching world history, 95–111
Arkansas, 9
Asian students, 65; Japanese American students, 77; opportunity for, 67; on tasks, 68
assassinations, 10; King, M. L., and, 11
assimilation, 25; rejection of, 26
asylum seekers, 75
Atlanta Compromise speech, 4
attitudes, 114–15; behavior and, 41–42; learning processes and, 41
Australia, 75
avoidance, 30

awareness, 15; reading and, 108; of self-image, 50
awe of the ancient, xiv
AYP. *See* Adequate Yearly Progress

Back to Africa movement, 7
Barton, Keith C., 51
Baudolino (Eco), 97–104
behaviors, 41–42; expectations and, 119–22
beliefs, 17, 105
Bell, Derrick, xvi
The Bell Curve (Herrnstein and Murray), 12
bigotry, 52
Bilingual Education Act (1968-2001), 12
Black Codes, 3
Black community, 47
Black Consciousness, 129–30; Garvey and, 7–8
Black Hawk War, 84
Black history, 46; Black teachers and, 56; terminology of, 52
Black History Week/Month, 8
Black students, 71–72
Black Studies discipline, 25
Black teachers, 56
boredom, 69, 70
brain, 138; research and, 42–44
Brazil, 37
Brown, John, 6
Brown v. Board of Education, 8–9
busing, 12

career, 60; considerations about, 61
categories, 90–91, 142; social categorization, 38
Central High school, 9
Chavis, John, 2
Cherokee Nation v. Georgia, 84
children, 69; language and, 40; needs of, 24

China, 53
Christianity, 2, 81
citizenship, 3; African Americans and, 6
Civil Rights Act (1964), 10
Civil Rights movement, xiv–xv, 8; reflection on, 92–93
Civil War (US), xii, 89; life after, 90
Clark, Kenneth, 10
classrooms, 31, 42, 59; conflicts in, 48; students of color and, 113–40
Clinton, Hillary, 11
cognitive factors, 29–44
Cold War, 9
The Coleman Report (1966), 11
collective memory, xiv–xv; multiculturalism and, 25
collectivist culture, 39
colonization, 81–82
colorism, 7
commemoration, xi
common identity, 20
communication, 115–16
communities, xv, 106; families and, 118
communities of color, xiv; Black community, 47; existence among, xv
conflation, 55
conflict, 76; in classrooms, 48; culture and, 75
Connecticut, 2
connection, 65, 106; post Civil War life and, 90
consciousness, 23; communities and, xv; historical consciousness, 23, 90–91; language and, 40. *See also* Black Consciousness
Constitution (US), 3
content, 69, 72; relevance of, 26
context, 57, 96–97
coping mechanisms, 23
cotton, 87, 88, 90
counterstories, 73–93, 123; of Native Nations, 81–82; of slavery, 85–87

Index ~ 155

countries, 72, 95; home and, 51. *See also specific countries*
Critical Race Theory (CRT), xvi, 73; role of, 100
Cullen, Countee, xiii
The Culturally Deprived Child (Riessman), 9
culturally responsive teaching, 47
culture, xv, 76; collectivist culture, 39; conflict and, 75; understanding and, 96
curiosity, 113–40
curriculum, 26; representation and, 71
Czarniawska, B., 78–79

data, 15, 24; collection of, 80; differences in, 109–10; education and, 32
de-constructive perspective, 40
deep learning, 31
deficit cultures, 9–10
deficit narratives, 81
degrees, 15
democracy, 1
deprivation, 36
diaspora, 24, 127; consequences of, 37; histories of, 7
dichotomy, 46
digital frameworks, 126–27
disclosure, xii
disconnection, 65
discourse, 73
discussion, 128; understanding and, 65–66
distortion, 83, 126
distractions, 62
dominant groups, xv
double historical consciousness, 23
Du Bois, W. E. B., 3–5, 16
Dunning, W. A., 6

Eco, Umberto, 97–104
education, 32; Coleman Report on, 11; denial of, 1–2; legislation and, 23; marginalization in, 52; motivation and, 29–30; Outcome Based Education, 13; scholars of, 78; shopping for, 50; since *Brown v. Board of Education*, 8–9. *See also specific types of education*
educational attainment, 35–36
educators, 93; expectations of, 114–15; language and, 40
Elementary and Secondary Education Act (ESEA), 10–11
Ellis Island, xiii
Emdin, C., 24
emotions, 66; learning and, 27
empire, xi
encoding, 43, 141
encouragement, 42
engagement, 20, 79, 106; alienation and, 61; anger and, 66; curiosity and, 113–40; extrinsic motivation and, 30; students and, 31
English as a Second Language (ESL), 14
Epstein, T., 22–23
eras, 107–8, 109–10
ESEA. *See* Elementary and Secondary Education Act
ESL. *See* English as a Second Language
Ethiopia, 53
ethnicity, 110
euphemisms, 16
Eurocentrism, 108–9; exceptionalism and, 104–5
exclusion, 1; Asian students and, 65; content and, 72; exclusionary stories, 5–6
exclusionary stories, 5–6
expectations, 69; behaviors and, 119–22; of educators, 114–15
experience, 25, 96, 126; anger and, 71; contrast with, 46; narratives and, 100; of racism, 86
extrinsic motivation, 29–30

Index

failure, 30–31
families, 118
fascism, 53
Faubus, Orval, 9
fear, 64; failure and, 30–31
feedback, 43–44
Fifteenth Amendments, 3
findings, 70–71
Fisher, D. R., 27
Fortune, T. Thomas, 4
Fourteenth Amendment, 3
Freeman, Alan, xvi
Freire, Paulo, 12
function, 18; histories and, 27
funding, 8; AYP and, 13; remedial programs and, 14

Garvey, Marcus, 7–8
General Certification of Secondary Education (GCSE), 52
Generation X, 57
Georgia, 93
Germany, 60
Gillborn, David, xvi
goals, 11, 16, 106, 138; career, 60; learning and, 32; motivation and, 50; self-esteem and, 35
Great Migration, 7
Great War, 7

Hampton Institute, 3
HBCUs. See Historically Black Colleges and Universities
Head Start, 10–11
hegemony, 5
heritage, 45
Herrnstein, R. J., 12
historians, 4; career as, 60
historical consciousness, typology for, 90–91
historical figures, 48, 49
Historically Black Colleges and Universities (HBCUs), 7–8
histories, 84, 129; alternative histories, 19; of diaspora, 7; of empire, xi; function and, 27; hidden histories, 51–53
history, 24, 60; distance from, 88; of history education, 1–16; identities and, 48–53; inadequacies and, 61–63; interest and, 53; for knowledge, 53–54; memory and, 46–48; ownership of, 89; perspective and, 55; students and, 21–22; students of color and, 45–57
history education: for African Americans, 1–16; in United States, xvii
history lessons, 55, 106; absorption in, 61; African Americans and, 22–23; alienation during, 68; anger and, 63; dislike of, 63; tools and, 50; values and, 137–38
the Holocaust, 60
Home Economics, 45
Howard University, 3; publications by, 7
Hughes, Langston, xiii

ICT. See Information and Communication Technology
ideas, 7, 17; decoding of students', 59–72; freedom as, 92; impact of, 74; motivation and, 101
identities, xv, 46; common identity, 20; formation of, xvii; history and, 48–53; religion and, 102–4; social groups and, 127–29
ideology, 105
ignorance, 54; counterstories of, 85–86; of histories, xi; White students and, 88
imagery, 51
impact, 62; of ideas, 74; social context and, 57
inadequacies, 61–63

inclusion, 24; content and, 72; involvement and, 37, 65; students and, 57
inclusive narratives, 18
independence, 37
Individuals with Disabilities Act, 13
inequalities, 20
influences, 23
information, xii; accumulation of, 18; efficacy and, 35; memory and, 43; processes for, 41; self and, 47
Information and Communication Technology (ICT), 122
in-service/pre-service teachers, 14–15; acknowledgment by, 99; teacher preparation programs, 47
integration, 9; busing and, 12
interactions, 39, 124
intercultural competence, 39
interdependence, 37, 106
interest, 64, 70; curiosity and, 67–68; history and, 53; in students, 118; White students, 71, 89
interviews, 45; insights from, 46
intrinsic motivation, 29–30
involvement, 67; inclusion and, 37, 65
Islam, 111
Italy, 53

Jackson, Andrew, 6
Japan, 77
Johnson, Lyndon B., 10; Vietnam War and, 12

Kennedy, John F., 10
King, Martin Luther, 11; activities about, 74
King, Rodney, 47
Kipling, Rudyard, 5
Kitayama, S., 36–37
knowledge, 118; history for, 53–54

Ladson-Billings, Gloria, xvi
language, xvii, 117–18; acquisition of self through, 40; self and, 79; value and, 38
laws, 62
learning, 132–33; multicultural students and, 29–44; outside of school, 56; ownership of, 83; students and, 17–27
learning difficulties, 66
learning processes, 41
Lee, Bruce, 76
legislation, 12–14; education and, 23; against schooling, 2
listening, 78
Los Angeles riots, 47

magazines, 62
Malcolm X, 47–48
Mandela, Nelson, 74–75
marginalization, 52, 106
Marks, R., 104–5
Markus, H. R., 36–37
material culture, 133–34
McKay, Claude, 7
memory, xii; attitude and, 41; differences in, 22; history and, 46–48; information and, 43; self and, 36; social categorization and, 38
mental challenge, 43
Mexico, 20
Milliken v. Bradley, 12
motivation, 29–30; arousal of, 36; differences in, 63–64; goals and, 50; ideas and, 101; motivational processes, 31–32; relevance and, 68
multicultural education, 21
multiculturalism, 25–27
multicultural students, 106; learning and, 29–44; profiles of, 59; work of, 79

Murray, C., 12
Myrdal, Gunnar, 16

NAACP. *See* National Association for the Advancement of Colored People
NAFTA. *See* North American Free Trade Agreement
names, xi
narrative analysis, xvi, 78; reflections and, 99; stories and, 96
narrative method, 78
narratives, 17, 81; action and, 18; Afrocentric Narratives, 23–25; children and, 40; experience and, 100; of students, xvi
Narratives in Social Science Research (Czarniawska), 78–79
National Association for the Advancement of Colored People (NAACP), 6
National Council for the Social Studies (NCSS), 15
National Defense Education act (1958), 9
nationality, 86
A Nation at Risk (1983), 12–13
Native Nations, 73; counterstories of, 81–82; White students and, 83–84
NCLB. *See* No Child Left Behind Act (2001)
NCSS. *See* National Council for the Social Studies
needs, 88; of children, 24
neglect, 19
neighborhoods, xiii
neuroscience, 43
neutrality, 56; perspective and, 57
New York Age newspaper, 4
Nixon, Richard, 12
No Child Left Behind Act (2001) (NCLB), 13

North America: colonization in, 81–82; settlers in, 75; slavery in, 1
North American Free Trade Agreement (NAFTA), 20

objectives, 122
Ohio, 2
opportunities, 25; for sharing, 67
Origins of the Modern World (Marks), 104–5
Outcome Based Education, 13
ownership, 67, 142; history and, 89; of learning, 83; terminology and, 86; of work, 32

participation, 43; participants and, 96; setting and, 80
patterns, 59; of findings, 70–71
pedagogy, 117; reform of, 23
Pedagogy of the Oppressed (Freire), 12
perceptions, 114; of self-efficacy, 49
performance, 10; affirmation of, 34
perspective, 22, 124; explanation and, 55–57; issue of, 125–26; of social constructionist, 38–40; White teachers and, 55
Phi Delta Pi Record, 47
Phrenology, 5
PL 94-142 (1975). *See* Individuals with Disabilities Act
Plessy v. Ferguson, 5–6, 8, 16
poetry, xiii, 126, 129; Kipling and, 5; Wheatley and, 2
possible selves, 36, 49–51
power, 54
practitioner research, 91
preparation, 47; prerequisites, 113–14
prerequisites, 113–14
pride, xiv, 48; survival and, 65
progressive multiculturalism, 26
Prohibition, 67

proverbs, 107
psychology, 33

Al Qaeda, 105

racism, 3, 52; apartheid and, 74–75; continuation of, 20; experience of, 86; neutrality and, 56; poetry and, 5; slavery and, 85, 92; systemic legacy of, 14
reading, 1, 62, 108; writing and, 122
Reality Pedagogy (Emdin), 24
Reconstruction period, xii
reform, 8; pedagogy and, 23
relationships, 116–17
relevance, 65; content and, 26; motivation and, 68
religion, 102–4, 111; Christianity and, 2, 81
remedial programs, 14
remembrance, xi
representation, xiv; curriculum and, 71; lack of/negative, 64–65; textbooks and, 26
research, xvii, 17; as brain based, 42–44; cross-cultural research, 39; Fisher and, 27; practitioner research, 91; questions for, 80–81; skills and, 66
respect, 89; acceptance and, 116
rewards, 32
Riessman, Frank, 9
riots, 10, 11; Los Angeles riots, 47
role models, 51
role-play, 66–67
Rüsen, Jörn, 90–91
Russia, 60

satisfaction, 60
Saxe, John Godfrey, 126
school, 2, 9; diversity in, 44; learning outside of, 56; after slavery, 5
Schools History Council Project, 69

segregation, 3; Civil Rights Act (1964) and, 10
self: acquisition of, xvii; information and, 47; language and, 79; memory and, 36; social constructionist and, 38–40
self-concept: age and, 34–35; Black self-concept, 36–37; development of, 38; nature of, 33; self-esteem and, 33–34
self-efficacy, 33; educational attainment, 35–36; perceptions of, 49
self-esteem: goals and, 35; self-concept and, 33–34
self-image, 33; awareness of, 50
self-reporting, 95
settings, 80
shame, 49, 84
Shaw University, 3
Shemilt, J., 69
silent observers, 79
skills, 45
slavery, 49, 130–32; colorism and, 7; counterstories of, 85–87; in North America, 1; racism and, 85, 92; school after, 5; survival and, 65; topic of, 52; White students and, 87–88
social constructionist, xvi–xvii; self and, 38–40
Social Darwinism, 6; survival of the fittest and, xiv
social groups, 127–29
social identity, 37–38
social science, 9
social studies, 111n1
society, 34, 70; imagery and, 51; understanding and, 54
The Souls of Black Folk (Du Bois), 4
South Africa: Mandela and, 74–75; Truth and Reconciliation Commission in, xiv

Soviet Union, 9. *See also* Russia
speeches, 4
Sputnik satellite, 9
stereotypes, 37
stimulation, 43
Stono Slave Rebellion, 1
stories, 48, 108; exclusionary stories, 5–6; majoritarian stories, 78, 88; narrative analysis and, 96
stress, 61; academic achievement and, 63
students, 11–12; disservice to, 47; engagement and, 31; history and, 21–22; ideas of, 59–72; inclusion and, 57; interest in, 118; learning and, 17–27; narratives of, xvi; self-reporting by, 95; in studies, 80
students of color, 21, 71; categories and, 91; classrooms and, 113–40; examination of past by, 73–93; history and, 45–57; Native Nations and, 81–82; reflections by, 92; slavery and, 85–87
studies, 18; interviewees in, 19; students in, 80
studying, 62; reasons for, *71*
subjects, 70
success, 38
surface learning, 31
surveys, 64; subjects and, 70
survival: pride in, 65; survival of the fittest, xiv
Swann v. Mecklenburg, 12
syllogism, 96

Tajfel, H., 37
talented tenth, 4
teacher preparation programs, 47
teachers: gatekeepers and, 20; perspective and, 55
teaching history, xii, 118; expectations and, 69; learning history and, 19–21; world history and, 95–111

technology, 51; achievement and, 52
terminology, 15–16; Black history as, 52; ownership and, 86
testing, 13, 134–35
textbooks, 21, 95, 110; distortion in, 83; representation and, 26
theoretical framework, xvi–xvii
theories, 24; motivation and, 29
Thirteenth Amendment, 3
Till, Emmett, xiii
Title 1, 10–11
Title IX (1972), 12
Tombs, Robert, 92
tools, 36; cultural tools, 18; history lessons and, 50; by Rüsen, 90–91
Trail of Tears, 83
travel, xiii
Trump, Donald, 20
trust, 116
truth, 55
Truth and Reconciliation Commission (South Africa), xiv
Tuskegee Institute, 3

understanding, 39, 142; action and, 46–48; culture and, 96; discussion and, 65–66; inclusive narratives and, 18; society and, 54
United Kingdom, 21; British culture in, 76
United States, 91; history education in, xvii; race relations in, 53, 92; trends in, 2–3

value, 34; history lessons, 137–38; judgments and, 89; language and, 38; opinions and, 67; prestige and, 54
Vietnam War, 12
voice, 18; agency and, 78; polyphony and, 27

Washington, Booker T., 3–5
websites, 127

Wheatley, Phillis, 2
White students, 69, 70; interests for, 71, 89; Native Nations and, 83–84; slavery and, 87–88
Whitney, Eli, 87
Wineburg, S., 69
Woodson, Carter G., 5; Black History Week/Month and, 8; ideas of, 7
Woodward, Harlan, 4
Woodward, Vann, 4
words, 59
world history, 95–111
worldview, 44
World War II, 76–77
writing, 1; freestyle, 73; of history, 24; reading and, 122

About the Author

Kay Traille taught history at secondary school and university level and guided preservice teachers for over three decades in a variety of settings from the urban United Kingdom to the southern United States. Her research centers on inclusion and diversity in history education, specifically how best to teach emotional and controversial histories.

www.ingramcontent.com/pod-product-compliance
Lightning Source LLC
Chambersburg PA
CBHW051812230426
43672CB00012B/2703